TESTIMONY

Mark Chadbourn

Emerald Eye

First published in this format in 2022 by Emerald Eye

ISBN: 978-0-9930302-2-2

Cover design by Eve Chadbourn

Photograph by Elizabeth Udall

Also by Mark Chadbourn:

The Age of Misrule trilogy
Science is failing. Magic is returning to the modern world…along with all the creatures of myth, legend and folklore.

World's End
Darkest Hour
Always Forever

The Dark Age trilogy
The world is reeling from the Age of Misrule. Dragons firebomb cathedrals. Shapeshifters stalk supermarkets. How can humanity survive?

The Devil in Green
The Queen of Sinister
The Hounds of Avalon

The Kingdom of the Serpent trilogy
The final act in the Age of Misrule, as the Brothers and Sisters of Dragons fight to the last.

Jack of Ravens
The Burning Man
Destroyer of Worlds

The Swords of Albion trilogy
Elizabethan spies fight to keep England safe from the supernatural threat of Faerie's Unseelie Court.

The Sword of Albion (US title: The Silver Skull)
The Scar-Crow Men
The Devil's Looking Glass

Writing as James Wilde:

Historical fiction. The rousing, bloody story of England's greatest hero, Hereward, the warrior, battling one thousand years ago.

Hereward
Hereward: The Devil's Army
Hereward: End of Days
Hereward: Wolves of New Rome
Pendragon
Dark Age
The Bear King

Preface

Strange faces appear on the floor of a house in a remote village in southern Spain. A ghost plane rises from the depths of Ladybower Reservoir on the Derbyshire Moors in England. The mummified hand of an English martyr is used to raise a Benedictine monk from a coma on the edge of death.

Odd stories. Perhaps unbelievable stories. Yet all of them were reported in British newspapers…just a tiny drop in the tidal wave of weirdness that sweeps over us every day of the year, all over the globe. In this age of high technology we like to believe we've left superstition…and the supernatural…far behind. But those tales, and thousands like them, reveal the truth.

Sometimes it seems the mundane, grey reality of our day-to-day lives peels back and we see what lies behind. It might be a tale whispered by a close friend in a shop or a pub, or we might even experience it ourselves, something we can't explain, appearing then disappearing in the blink of an eye. Often it gives us a brief feeling of wonder, almost a religious transcendence. Occasionally, it can fill us with the deepest dread.

Our rational mind tells us we are at the mercy of strictly defined rules that allow no place for the paranormal. What, then, of the testimonies of everyday people: doctors, lawyers, secretaries, shop workers and office managers? People who are not unduly gullible, who live their lives fully in the 'real' world yet who have experienced, something that cannot be explained away by science? Sometimes, in the quiet of our lonely rooms, we look deep inside ourselves and feel that life is strange, that the rules aren't so rigid, and that things and thoughts and happenings creep around the shadows of our lives yet never enter the light. We would never admit it in public. But in our hearts, we *fear* …

I am a writer of fiction. I am comfortable with creating the fantastic in my head. I am also, by trade, a journalist, steeped in that profession's culture of cynicism, used to operating in that grey, mundane world where everything has a rational explanation. So when I first encountered the Rich family and Heol Fanog, their picturesque house deep in the Welsh countryside, I approached their tale with a healthy scepticism. Yes, strange, inexplicable things did happen in the world. But their story was too unbelievable – too terrifying – to be true. The truly horrifying, on a spiritual level, only happens in novels.

What you are about to read is not fiction. It is fact. Then again, we are told there are no facts, just different perspectives of the same view: subjective, coloured by personal beliefs, doubts, fears. Yet when two of those perspectives are aligned, we start to get closer to the heart of the matter. When three, four or five are in tune we can be pretty sure we have got as close as we can get to the truth of an event.

Many people of varying degrees of credulity, differing ages, sex and religious persuasion, are convinced something beyond the bounds of reason happened at Heol Fanog between November 1989 and June 1995. Something supernatural. Something evil.

This wasn't a simple haunting. This was human life pushed to the limit by a malignant force that exhibited a terrifying sentience, or so it seemed. A battle not only for the sanity of Heol Fanog's bewildered, increasingly distressed residents, but ultimately for their very souls.

I was drawn to the story of the Rich family by an article that appeared in the *Independent*, a newspaper not renowned for fantastic supposition. It told of a house where strange things happened, where electricity was drained from the system for no reason. It also hinted at other, darker things, which it decided, in its wisdom, to leave well alone. I, not being particularly wise, wanted to know more. I rang the Riches and chatted to them about their experiences, ostensibly to write an article for a magazine, but also because my curiosity was piqued.

As Bill Rich and I talked, I realized the *Independent* had only scratched the surface of what had happened in that house. There was an interesting story to tell on many levels.

A story not just of the supernatural but of raw, human emotion as ordinary people struggled to cope in the face of madness, of how lives can be unbalanced by the real world and those who claim to be spiritual saviours.

But at its heart it *is* a story of the supernatural. If you accept all that is documented herein, Heol Fanog could be the most haunted house in Britain. That would be frightening enough, but there is more. Much more. The people who give their testimonies in this book will unveil one of the most startling cases of the paranormal ever to be documented, a case which starts with a haunting and carries on into the shadows. Its final destination is somewhere very dark and terrible.

Remember: it is a true story.

Chapter 1

At first they thought everything was all right.

Bill Rich gripped the wheel of the Volvo as he negotiated the winding lanes through the Welsh hill country from Brecon town. On the roof rack, the wardrobe rumbled from side-to-side, threatening to pitch off. The roads were barely wide enough for one car. The twists and turns made it impossible to tell what lay even a few feet ahead. Tall, thick trees clustered tight on either side, but occasionally a break allowed a breath-taking vista across the Usk valley towards the Black Mountains rising up ominously in the distance.

The day was framed in their memories like a Monet or a Gauguin: hazily seen fields of bright green, half-glimpsed splashes of red in the branches of rowans, a touch of yellow far off against a sprawling hedge. An azure sky puffed with white, and the shadowy purple peaks of the Brecon Beacons were an inspirational backdrop to that warm May day in 1989.

'I still can't believe we've got it.' Bill glanced at his girlfriend and Liz smiled and nodded with a mixture of relief and contentment. Physically, they were almost opposites: shadow and light. Bill, dark and intense behind a thick beard, his blue eyes cautious and thoughtful. Liz, long, fair hair, tall and slender with an open, smiling face. He was forty-three, thirteen years older than Liz, but deeper ties bound them.

'How much further, Billy?' From the back seat, Bill's fourteen-year-old son from his first marriage thrust his head between the two adults.

'Not far, Laurence. Calm down. There's plenty of space for you to burn off energy where we're going. Not like back in Llan Tallyn.' Bill was glad to turn his back on the terraced house they had finally left behind that morning. Not so long ago it had seemed perfect but now it was filled with too many bad memories. 'You'll be able to stand in the garden and shout your head off to your heart's content and nobody will hear you.'

'No neighbours?'

'You'll have to travel at least half a mile to find the nearest one. There's only about five houses in the whole area.'

And that was what they wanted: splendid isolation. No prying eyes judging their lives, no tongues wagging over garden fences. They'd had their fill of that during the last few months.

Turning down an even tinier lane, which wound steeply past a farm, then a bungalow, Bill searched for signs in the hedgerow that would tell him when to slow down. Even when they were upon it, their destination rested silently behind an impenetrable wall of trees, letting the modern world pass it by.

Then, suddenly, it was there.

A pool of shadow from the tall trees permanently engulfed the crossroads, but Bill knew the right-hand road was the drive to the house. He swung the Volvo up to the wide wooden gate and peered through trees.

'There it is. Heol Fanog.'

Heol Fanog – Road to the Peaks, in Welsh – a fine stone house set in three acres of glorious countryside. It wasn't wholly theirs – they could afford only to rent such a grand place – but it was the perfect setting to start their new life.

Suddenly quiet after the chatter of the first part of the journey, they walked slowly up the hard earth drive until they stood before the house. It was long and thin, converted from an ancient barn in the fifties; they could still see where the new cement had been used to build up the top to support the slate roof.

They stared at it for a moment before Laurence suddenly peeled off with a laugh and disappeared into the thick undergrowth. Liz took a step closer to Bill and slipped an arm around his waist. 'Listen,' she said.

He cocked his head. 'I can't hear anything.'

'Exactly. It's perfect.' She rested her head on his shoulder, still watching the house. 'There's something else. Can you feel it?' She closed her eyes and said again dreamily, 'Can you *feel* it? The moment we stepped through the gate, it seemed like we were moving into another world. I had this wonderful feeling of serenity and security, as if nothing can touch us here. I feel like there's a dome over the whole house protecting us.'

'You know, I felt that too.' Bill laughed. 'I thought it was just me being silly.'

They could hear Laurence whooping and hollering as he crashed among the trees. Liz took Bill's hand and started to pull him in the other direction. 'Come on.'

She led him off the drive and through bushes and grass into the thickest copse. Underneath the canopy, in the cool shadows, a carpet of bluebells shone. When they were far enough from the drive, Liz stopped and kissed Bill passionately.

'Sealed with a kiss,' she said. 'A new life in the shelter of our magic dome at the heart of nature.'

Bill placed a hand on her bare stomach. 'You think the baby will like it here?'

'The baby will love it here.' She stroked her belly. "He doesn't a say in the matter so he'll just have to trust us.'

For a few minutes they were silent, listening to the breeze in the trees. When the echoes of Laurence's excited calls stirred them, they made their way back to the drive.

He was standing near the house, pointing off into the trees. Before Bill could ask what he had found, the excited teenager darted into the greenery. Bill followed his path down an incline until he found the boy standing in a clearing, surveying some strange stone ruins. They covered a wide area – crumbling columns, low broken walls, a memory of rooms, almost obscured by long, yellow grass, brambles and climbing ivy.

'What's that?' Laurence studied the piles of stone, trying to picture what it had once been. His exuberance ebbed away.

'The ruins of the old house – the original Heol Fanog. It dates back to medieval times, apparently. When the builders were converting the barn, they used the stone from here because the old place had fallen into such a state of disrepair. Don't go in amongst those ruins, Laurence. Those stacks don't look too safe and there's a cellar underneath here somewhere.'

'No,' Laurence said in a subdued voice. 'I don't think I will.

*

It started in such a simple, pleasant way. Bill and Liz had found the home at the culmination of a very difficult period for both of them. It was just right for all their needs, but it was one thing in particular that attracted them: a forty-foot room over the garage-cum-barn, which Bill wanted to use as his studio. An artist of some note, he had earned himself a good living from his work, and he was keen to have a place of his own where he could devote himself to his 'masterpiece'.

Painting was Bill's driving ambition. Although he had an early flirtation with art, he only discovered his passion for it after spending much of his life searching for something that would fulfil him. Born in Dorset to an ex-serviceman who had a strong dislike of creative people, he attended Ruskin College of Fine Art in Oxford at sixteen, until he was expelled for an affair with the head's daughter. Heartbroken at being forced to give up his studies, he signed up on a whim with the Royal Navy's 845 Squadron and headed out to Borneo. It wasn't long before he realized he had made the wrong decision. Jumping ship, he disappeared into the depths of the jungle. While trying to stay one step ahead of the authorities, he headed for Sarawak in the south of the island where he was given shelter by a local tribe of head-hunters. Over a period of weeks, Bill ran around in a loincloth, following all the tribe's customs in a desperate rebellion against the regimented forces' life. But as he began to adapt to his simple existence, the navy tracked him down and he spent six weeks in a cell on HMS Bulwark *en route* to Britain, where he was court-martialled.

With a desire to travel instilled by his experiences in Borneo, Bill headed straight out to Australia where, from 1975, he established a booming business painting nightclubs and boutiques. After a few months, he realized his job wasn't fulfilling him. He dropped everything and made his way to Finucane Island off the west coast to join a protest against mineral extraction at an Aboriginal holy place. Bill spent many weeks with the Aborigines where he felt at home with their quiet, spiritual life, and eventually it helped him reconnect with his original desire to be an artist. His first paintings in many years were developed in a new style with an Aboriginal influence, and were exhibited by the Alliance Française in Melbourne. But his plans to return to England and take up painting full-time were disrupted when he fell in love and decided to marry. The responsibilities of being a husband and father took over.

After sixteen years of marriage, Bill's first wife Denise left him for another man. When she walked out, Laurence had chosen to remain with his father. Bill was thrust into an unfamiliar domestic regime and forced to learn quickly for his son's sake. Denise's affair and subsequent departure had come as a complete shock to him, and the stress of suddenly finding himself alone and a single parent drove him to seek medical help. When that failed he was advised by a friend to see a herbalist in Cardiff. That turned out to be Liz.

*

Bill Rich' testimony: 'With the Aborigines I was seeing something that I couldn't quite connect with, but I could marvel at its simplicity. Having read of similar types of society in other parts of the world, I was instantly attracted to their life in the primitive places, the quiet places. By the time I got back to this part of the world, part of me had to accept what I was, but there was also part of me that wanted to get back there because they know what is proper, what is *real*. We don't know it. The commercial world we find here in the West is not only becoming terribly unattractive, it has been going that way for some considerable time – built on wealth and fashion and violence.

'From the experience, I knew that I really wanted to become a painter. That was the only thing I could see. I certainly couldn't see the nine-to-five for me. I knew there was something building up within me that was going to come out, and I was waiting for that time. In retrospect, it would probably have been better if I had been on my own, instead of getting married. I should have been stuck in a cell waiting for that moment when that image, that creative time was there. I have always regarded life as terribly boring. I need to be excited in some way, usually through the imagination… then I can put it down on canvas.

'After moving into Heol Fanog, I was full of enthusiasm. It wasn't just the realization that we'd come from a small village location in a terraced house. We had actually come to an artist's dream. I had plenty of money in the bank. There was this forty-foot studio. I was starting to find as an artist, at my age of forty-three and not getting any younger, that this was the place it was going to happen. The images were starting to come, I was excited, the tingling was within me, the brushes were there. All paid for, all ready to go. There was certainly this feeling that if I don't do something quick with my painting, I'm going to be forgotten.

'Yet despite that, my prime concern was not my work, it was Laurence's little mind, and his life, and how we were going to cope. Denise's leaving was such a terrible shock. I knew it must have affected him badly. People can become terribly ambitious until something like that happens in life. All my energies were directed towards making sure Laurence was going to be OK. When I met Liz – even though she was right for me – I didn't want him thinking he was going to be pushed out. I was more in love with him than I was with Liz and he only had to say go away and she would have done. I would have given up everything for Laurence.

‘From my own perspective, from the first time I saw her I knew that there was something in Liz I wanted to find more about. I still feel the same way, so I know it was a good decision at that time. After six years, and after going through the horrible situation, we find we love each other more than ever.

‘Everything that has happened in that house that was beyond explanation, I would want to understand it, even though I couldn’t understand it. On one level, and at the earliest stage, it was interesting. In the end, it was frightening. It had every possible hit on the emotional system. It affected how you thought, how you slept. If Liz and I hadn’t been strong as a couple – if we had allowed it to split us up – we would never have survived. It was just the love that we had as people that kept us going.

Although Liz and Bill are alike in many ways, her life could not have been more different. While Bill travelled extensively, Liz stayed, apart from a brief period, in Wales. While Bill interacted with the cultures he encountered, Liz withdrew into herself. Her upbringing in Cowbridge, Glamorgan, was tempestuous, and she felt she never really fitted in. After failing her eleven-plus her mother and father sent her to a convent in the hope that the discipline would bring her into line. Liz instantly rebelled and by the time she was fourteen she was spending her free time with hippies, rockers and artists, drinking and dabbling in drugs. Her family sent her to live with her brother in Leicester and then to Cardiff School in a final, desperate attempt to straighten her out, but in her own words she ‘went from bad to worse’. She came out with just two O levels – in English language and pottery – and then she enrolled in a local technical college to train as a nursery nurse. By this time her outrageous lifestyle had devolved into a constant round of heavy drinking, and she began to put on weight.

Her attempt to diet became increasingly strained until finally she slipped into anorexia, a debilitating condition that affected her for twelve years and almost ruined her life. She became a recluse, bingeing then forcing herself to be sick for up to ten times a day. Although she stopped her drinking and drug-taking she became hooked on laxatives, which she thought would keep her weight down. Her condition deteriorated until her hair was falling out and her teeth were loose. Yet Liz never gave up on the illness. She sought a range of medical help, but nothing seemed to work, and she even attempted to break out of her reclusive lifestyle by taking a job in a nursery, but she was so constantly tired it was only a matter of time before she was sacked.

At her lowest ebb, Liz ran away to the Mediterranean where she spent months touring round the Greek islands. By the time she returned to Britain, Liz was depressed and suffering with ringworm and psittacosis because the anorexia had depleted her immune system. All conventional medical help had failed her. Finally she saw a gypsy herbalist in Cardiff who helped her control her condition enough to get out and about. That small success convinced her to train as a herbalist and, still anorexic and fighting it every day, she opened up for business in Cardiff.

Bill was sent to her for treatment for his own depression, and it didn't take long for them to recognize their attraction. But Bill was aware of the mountainous emotional and psychological difficulties he faced trying to bring Liz into their lives.

*

Their first encounter with something strange happened soon after their meeting. Bill had decided the best way to build bonds between Laurence and Liz was to take a holiday together in Egypt. It had always been Laurence's dream to visit the land of the Pharaohs and Bill knew his son's excitement at seeing that dream fulfilled would put him more at ease in the new family set-up.

One of the first sites on Laurence's agenda was the Pyramid of Cheops. Bill and Liz were excited at the prospect of the visit too, and they were all eager to follow the dark passageways into the pyramid's heart. Setting off early to beat the tourist rush, they were alone when they ventured into the enormous pyramid. It was chill and dank away from the scorching desert sun and their journey was slow along the cramped corridor that led to the burial chamber.

Liz was the first to reach their destination. But as she stood alone in the stark room she saw something that baffled her. Tiny lights like lasers shimmered among the walls, although there was no mechanism that could have caused them. Anxiously, she asked Bill and Laurence if they could see them too. They couldn't, but she could tell instantly that they were uneasy. Liz asked what was wrong and Bill replied nervously, 'I don't know. I can feel something.' Laurence nodded in agreement.

A second later, they all felt a presence in the room with them. Nothing was visible, but an irrational terror gripped them all simultaneously as if their lives were at risk. In an instant, they were scrambling wildly along the corridor and they didn't stop until they were out in the sun.

As they rested near the entrance and tried to understand what had happened to them, an American tourist asked Bill what it was like inside.

'Fucking horrible,' he replied.

Back in England, their experience wasn't forgotten, but it slipped into the background as their relationship developed. Laurence didn't approve, but he accepted. The first thing on the agenda was a new place to live. The old end-of-terrace house was filled with raw memories of Denise, and their landlady was convinced Bill was having an affair while his wife was away – she couldn't seem to grasp that Denise had left *him*. Rented properties in Brecon were hard to come by; the picturesque national park is a land of holiday homes, where it's more lucrative to rent to tourists than locals.

When they heard of Heol Fanog it was a moment of pure serendipity. They were at their lowest ebb, desperate to move out, unable to find anywhere. But there it was, well away from gossiping neighbours, peaceful, pleasing on the eye – they were hooked from the first time they saw it. There were other people interested, of course, and Bill and Liz were terrified they wouldn't get it. Luckily, the landlord found an affinity with Bill's love of art and then they had to wait only for the current tenant to decide when she was leaving. During the limbo period, and still afraid it would slip through their fingers, Bill and Liz would visit Heol Fanog while the tenant was away, to sit in the garden and dreamily plan what they would do there. In their minds it became a powerful totem to their formation of a new, happy life. At that time they got their first inkling of that magical, protective dome. They wanted Heol Fanog and it wanted them; it was a match made in heaven.

Two years away from that moment, as Bill Rich spoke of that tremendous sense of peace and serenity in a disbelieving voice, he would hear the words: ‘Yes, I’m sure it was like that. That was the welcoming party.’

Liz Rich’s testimony: ‘I was desperately lonely and screwed up. When I went to the Mediterranean, I really thought I could leave the anorexia behind, but it followed me. I couldn’t shake it off. It had its claws in me and whatever I tried to do to shake it off it just clung on tighter. I went to the health farms to try to get rid of it. What it is, and I know that now, is you’re desperate to find unconditional love. I wanted someone to love me for me, not for what I could give to them or for what I should be, but for me. Anorexia was the way it seemed to come out in me. Dreadful. It’s a long time, twelve years.

‘There was no one who could help. I went to homeopaths, hypnotherapists. I tried very hard. I was manic about exercise. I’d run about four miles a night. I’d work out in gyms. It’s like there a bloody demon in you and you’re trying to get rid of it and it’s eating away at you. But it’s all to do with love and being needed and being made to be indispensable. You have to have that. Because if you’re indispensable you have to watch out you don’t… die. And that is the answer to it

‘It went the day I met Bill and that was very weird. When he came to the clinic, he invited me out to lunch. I thought, Yeah I quite like you. But lunch! I thought, I could always get drunk and not eat anything. But it went and that was because there was love. There wasn’t judgement. It was just: Here’s Liz. I love her. She loves me. And I was so needed. And it went. And Bill didn’t even know I had it. He just thought I was very thin. Now I don’t think about it. I just eat, like everybody else.’

*

They trailed through the house in a state of wonder, as if they were seeing it for the first time. The entrance was through the garage-cum-barn, an area that reeked of age; even though the conversion was only forty years old, the barn that provided the shell dated back hundreds of years. There was a step up into the hallway, where wooden stairs rose up to the first floor; they were wide enough for three people to walk abreast. Off the hallway was a toilet. Beyond it was a small, dark kitchen with flagged floors, and through that was the lounge in the extension that had been built when the barn was converted, the brightest room in the house with windows on two walls.

They clattered excitedly up the stairs and swung open doors to exclaim, 'This will be our room,' or 'This will be the baby's room,' or 'This will be my room, but I want to decorate it myself.'

And then they came to the final room. Bill went in first and stood in the centre of the room, trying to imagine it as it had been in his dreams. The landlord's furniture was piled up to the ceiling and it was a home to a startling array of spiders, but the potential was obvious: his studio. There had never been space for him to paint in the old house, but here there was room for massive canvases, all his oils and brushes, chairs to sit and think. After years of holding the urge in, he could finally give it vent.

There was also enough space to work on his booming business, providing intricately painted boxes and small works of art for the gift market. Interest had been building up across America and Europe and the money was rolling in.

He turned towards Liz, who was standing in the doorway. 'I'm going to do great things here,' he said. 'I can feel it. I can't wait to get started.'

Liz smiled and nodded. She knew how much they all had been repressing his creative side while he struggled to cope with the marriage break up and maintain a home for Laurence.

He leaned against the wall and looked out of the dusty panes into the sun-drenched back garden. 'I spent all my life wandering, trying to find different things, jobs, business deals… always searching for something,' he said quietly. 'And then when I picked up a brush and sat alone in front of that blank canvas, I knew I'd found it. This is me, Liz. Everything I am is wrapped up in painting. I *have* to do it.'

'I understand, you know I do.' Liz gave his shoulder a squeeze. 'This is the right place, Bill. You've got space and time. You'll do your best work here. You'll find your masterpiece, I know you will.'

They gave each other a hug and then gathered up their strength to complete the move.

The summer passed too quickly. It seemed a blur of walks and dinner parties and horseplay in the sun, all of it preserved on a rented video camera. Bill and Liz were keen to have lots of animals around them; it seemed a vital part of the rural life they were creating for themselves. Bill had always wanted a pig, so one day in early summer they toured the local farms until they found one that caught their eye. They called her Lucinda Ragwort Rigland, and although she ran off shortly after arriving she soon returned and became an integral part of the household, lying in front of the stove in the kitchen like a guard dog. The big garden was a problem to keep under control, especially with Bill's increasing workload, so their next purchase was two sheep to keep the grass down. They disappeared overnight, so then the Riches bought some goats only to discover they don't eat grass. Still, Liz quickly became attached to them.

Though as irritable as any displaced teenager could be, Laurence assimilated into the new routine with remarkable ease. He couldn't find it within himself to call Liz 'mum', but he did begin to treat her as a big sister. The business was rolling and picking up speed; orders were flooding in. For the first time as a family, the Riches felt blessed. They had enough cash to live almost as they pleased and the setting for their work and play was idyllic.

One day towards the end of summer Bill made an odd discovery while ransacking a drawer full of invoices. The first one he pulled out was a bar bill for the last meal he bought Liz before they moved into Heol Fanog. It was for £6.66. The second invoice was from a supermarket where they stocked up on supplies for the house. It showed a total of £66.60.

'Hey,' he called to Liz in the kitchen. 'I think we're jinxed.' When she came through to the living room, he showed her the receipts with a grin. '666. The number of the beast. And do you remember the registration on that black Volvo that nearly rammed us when we were going to get the furniture for the move?'

'Sure. BST 666. I remember what you said at the time. It stood for Beast 666.' She laughed. 'Spooky!'

Bill screwed up the invoices and threw them in the bin. It was several months before they thought about them again.

The glorious atmosphere continued. They married on 28 September 1989, when Liz was heavily pregnant. They were both pleased that Laurence enjoyed the day and their respective families got on well.

The first shadow fell across their lives as autumn approached.

Liz's testimony: 'I was really excited when we moved into Heol Fanog because I was three months pregnant. It was the first baby, and because I'd had anorexia for twelve years I thought I'd never possibly be able to have children. I went for an amniocentesis test and it came back that there was something wrong, so then they sent me for a scan in Abergavenny and they found it was gastroschisis, which is where the baby's bowels and other internal organs come out of its body. So it's safe while it's in you, in the waters, but the moment it comes out, you don't know what the hell's going to come out, basically. They told me to have an abortion. I said I wasn't willing to have an abortion – I wouldn't have one. I remember lying in our bedroom saying to Bill, "I can't make friends with this baby because I don't know what the hell I've got in me anymore." I blamed myself so much because I'd had anorexia. I thought there must have been a link between twelve years of that and this peculiar one in every half a million babies.

'When he was born it was worse than they thought. I didn't see it. I had him a month early by Caesarean. He had his bowels, testicles, kidneys – everything – inside out. I knew he was alive, but I didn't see anything. They wrapped him up in clingfilm to keep him wet and they did, I think, an eight-hour operation to put everything back in that had come out. An amazing surgeon, that guy. And then he went into intensive care and was put on a respirator for a couple of days.

'I couldn't quite get a grip on the fact that I had a baby. I hadn't got the baby in me and I hadn't got him with me, so It didn't make sense. One nurse came up and said, "There's a problem with his toe. It's going black. We'll have to amputate his foot." I though, Shit. And that was the time I broke. There were floods of tears and everything was chaos because they said it was haematoma and it would just spread. So then I treated him with homeopathic medicine. This was while he was in the incubator and the doctors kicked up a fuss about all the sugar in homeopathic tablets, but I knew what I was doing. It worked and the toe was saved. All he's got now is a very bent big toe.'

Ben was born on 20 October 1989 and when Liz finally got him home to Heol Fanog it seemed like she had won three striking victories against fate: she had got pregnant in the first place, despite all the odds; Ben had survived the gastroschisis when the hospital authorities had wanted to abort him; and Liz had saved his foot when the doctors were sure the only way to save him was to amputate.

Still, despite their good fortune, the strain on both of them, and Liz in particular, was starting to tell. With the usual rigours of dealing with a newborn, it soon became obvious the added level of tension in their lives was there to stay for a while. Ben slept in a cradle next to Bill and Liz's bed in their room above the lounge, in the newest part of the house. Laurence's room was next door.

The volume of work was so great Bill couldn't devote as much time as he would have liked to his painting, but he did manage to clear the landlord's furniture to the back of the workshop and hang a six-foot by four-foot canvas in the centre, with a light above. He set his oils and brushes on a table nearby, ready for that moment when he could finally begin.

As winter approached, Heol Fanog lost some of the appeal it had radiated during the sunshine days of summer. Stripped of their leaves, the trees that clustered around the house seemed black and foreboding; they were tall and old and prevented much of the weak light reaching the house. Even on the brightest days, the small windows in the oldest part of the house created a natural gloom. There was also a chill that was hard to dispel on the coldest days, despite the oil-fired central heating. The house had little insulation and the windows were old and badly fitted. Outside, the peaks moved from purple, like an old bruise, to slate grey verging on black, as the clouds lowered overhead. Yet even then, the mood in the house was bright and optimistic.

*

It was around midnight on a cold, dark night in late November. Bill and Liz made love, and afterwards, breathless and trembling from the exertion, Bill felt a sudden pang of guilt. He buried his face in Liz's hair so he could whisper in her ear. 'I hope Laurence didn't hear anything,' he said. 'I don't want to upset him. Do you think he heard?'

Liz strained to hear any sound from the next room. The house was silent. 'I don't know. We were noisy – '

'I'll look in on him in a while. I'm just nipping down to the toilet.'

Next to them, the baby stirred and grizzled. 'Here we go, time for another feed,' Liz sighed.

Bill slipped out of the bedroom on to the cold landing, still concerned about Laurence. Although his son got on well with Liz, Bill was aware of the deep-seated problems that still remained.

Laurence had bottled up much of the shock and anguish he felt at suddenly finding himself living alone with his father, and Bill could sense all those negative emotions seething away inside his son; he didn't want to do anything that would compact the problem. That meant being with Liz, but not being too demonstrative, trying to pretend she was not a replacement for Laurence's mother, when in Bill's heart she had taken Denise's place long ago.

He paused outside his son's door, but he couldn't hear anything within, and then he tiptoed along the wooden landing and down the stairs to the toilet. It was icy cold in the dark hall and his breath plumed around him. As everyone was in bed, he left the door open while he relieved himself.

As he emptied his full bladder, his thoughts began to drift: to Liz upstairs feeding the baby and how happy she made him feel; to Laurence asleep in his bed and Bill's hopes that his son wouldn't suffer because of the new family situation; and then to his work, his painting, and the ache he felt to create something powerful and long-lasting.

The noise erupted somewhere above his head, like gunshots in the midnight still of the house. Bill started suddenly, and put one hand on the wall to support himself. It sounded like someone in hobnail boots pounding along the landing. Crash-crash-crash-crash-crash, then nothing.

Someone was about to come down the stairs. 'What the fuck is happening?' Bill muttered. Unconsciously, he swung the toilet door shut so he wouldn't be seen. When there were no further footsteps, Bill felt a brief moment of incomprehension and then slowly he guessed what it must have been.

'Laurence,' he sighed wearily.

His son had heard their lovemaking and he was showing his disapproval with the unfocused anger of a teenager. He would have to go in, talk to him and calm him, repeat the familiar mantra that everything would be all right, Liz wasn't replacing his mother, that they cared for each other, but that Laurence always came first.

Bill hurried upstairs and slipped into Laurence's room. It was pitch black. He moved forward quietly until he could see his son lying in bed. His breathing was regular; he was fast asleep. Bill's worries about Laurence were suddenly replaced by an uncharacteristic anxiety he couldn't quite explain. If it wasn't Laurence, then who had run along the landing so noisily?

Liz was still sitting up in bed feeding the baby. Ben sucked at the breast calmly; they both looked peaceful and undisturbed.

Bill waited for Liz to ask what the noise was, but when she simply smiled at him, he said 'Did you hear that?'

She put a finger to her lips to quiet him so he didn't disturb the baby. 'What?' she whispered.

Bill shook his head in disbelief. 'Lord, it sounded like the roof was falling in. Somebody running along the landing… in boots, it sounded like. I was in the toilet, so I was right underneath it.'

Liz looked at him blankly.

The anxiety swelled within him and he started to babble. 'I thought it was Laurence… I thought he heard us making love… I thought… I checked in on him. He was asleep. I –'

There was a note of worry in Liz's curious expression. 'I didn't hear a thing, Bill.'

Bill stepped out of the bedroom and looked down the dark corridor. Moonlight broke briefly through the thick clouds and filled the landing with a silvery illumination that glistened on the frosted panes. He listened carefully, holding his breath. The house was still. Nothing moved.

Nervously, he edged back into the bedroom and looked at Liz for an answer. 'What the hell was it?'

Down the years, Bill can't forget that moment. 'The shutters came down overnight,' he says.

*

Bill's testimony: 'I never used to believe in ghosts, these things, ever. I simply held an open mind. It was possible these things hadn't happened to me. I was an agnostic. But that night it was almost as if the good weather had changed inexplicably to bad weather, like a storm in the tropics. It was so quick – one minute from those footsteps, we were in darkness. It just happened as if someone was unveiling something. It was a short, sharp shock.'

*

Liz's testimony: 'The presence made itself known. The atmosphere started to change. There was a lot of fear then. I've always been terrified of ghosts and things like that, really terrified of them, and the thought that I was living in a house with something like that in it, it terrified me. And then of course when I heard them…'

Chapter 2

Overnight the house seemed to change. The thick stone walls appeared to press in on all sides until every room felt half the size, and a house that had seemed almost too big was now oppressively claustrophobic. In the brief, cold hours before dawn, Heol Fanog had also grown noticeably darker; they all commented on it. Even when the lights were on they never seemed to fill the house with the illumination that made it seem such a golden place in those summer months. It was more than just the bleak, grey winter without; it was like something was leaching the light so that an omnipresent gloom lay in every corner.

The next morning Bill and Liz didn't discuss the mysterious footsteps. It was something lost in that hazy night world which seemed ridiculous in the light of day. There were too many other things to think about – the baby, the orders for work that were piling up on the dresser in Bill's studio, a service on the car, a trip to the supermarket.

They took their breakfast around the kitchen table as they always did. Both of them were in a strangely dark, depressive mood, and although they didn't discuss it with each other, they both felt weary as if they hadn't slept at all. Bill munched on a piece of toast. Liz nursed the baby. They both shivered visibly at the same time.

'Are you cold?' Liz asked.

Bill nodded. 'It's very chilly today isn't it? Wouldn't be surprised if there was snow on the way. I'll turn the heating up.' He leaned across to the boiler and adjusted the thermostat. 'Where's Laurence?'

'Still in his room. You don't expect him to get up before eleven at a weekend, do you? He needs his beauty sleep, that boy.'

'He's been nagging me to redecorate his room. Or rather, to allow *him* to redecorate his room. I guess he wants to exert his independence, like all good, rebellious teenagers.'

'It'll be good for him, a place that's really his own. Are you going to give him some money for paint?'

'I'll sort it out later.' Bill settled back in his chair and finished his toast. 'You know, I think I've got an idea for a painting.'

'Is this going to be the masterpiece?'

'It came to me in a flash, this perfect image.' His eyes grew dreamy and faraway, a sign Liz always associated with the creative spirit. Briefly, she saw something else in his face, darker, more puzzling. He looked at her. 'Don't ask me to describe it to you. You'll just have to wait and see – when I can find the time to start work on it.'

'So *is* it the special one?'

'Every painting should be special to an artist.' He smiled. 'We'll see.'

There was a crunch of pebbles and frosted earth as the post van pulled up on to the rough driveway outside the gate, its red and yellow the only splash of colour in the landscape. Bill wandered out to meet the postman and returned with a couple of letters, one a bank statement, and the other a brown envelope stamped with the logo of Swalec, South Wales Electricity. Bill opened the bank statement first.

'Ben has done remarkably well, hasn't he?' Liz said, as she looked deep into the baby's eyes. 'And we haven't had any jealousy from Laurence. We've been very lucky.'

'Hmmm.' Bill put down the bank statement and opened the electricity bill.

'Do you think we should have any more?'

'Hmmm?'

'I said –'

'Good Lord!' Bill was staring at the bill incredulously.

'What is it? A little more than we expected?'

'A little more!' he said, outraged. 'It's £750… for a quarter! We'd have to have been powering every house for a couple of square miles to run up that amount.'

'They must have made a mistake.'

'That's an understatement.' Liz could see the first glimmer of anger in Bill's face. 'If they think we're going to pay that, then they've got another thought coming.' He threw the bill on to the table in disgust. 'I'll call them first thing Monday to sort it out.'

It was irritating, but mundane and easily forgotten; more important matters were already filling their minds. The bill lay on the kitchen table for the whole of the weekend without anyone realising its true significance.

*

A thundering along the landing and down the stairs brought back disturbing memories of the previous night. As they both flinched, they glanced at each other and knew they were thinking the same thing. Their relief was palpable as Laurence's head bobbed in the kitchen door, a pale face topped by a shock of brown hair.

'How are you doing, lad?' Bill asked cheerily, but the moment the words left his mouth he could tell there was something wrong. Laurence's face was pinched, scowling. 'Something wrong?' Bill said.

'No,' Laurence snapped. He glared at Liz and the baby for a moment and then started to retreat into the hall.

'It doesn't sound like it,' Bill said ironically.

Laurence's face was furious as he thrust it back into the doorway. 'I said there's nothing wrong!'

Bill had a sudden fear that Laurence *had* heard him making love with Liz the previous night. Had he been brooding all night about his mother and the break-up? If so, Bill could forgive Laurence's tone; he knew the bitterness and anger that could come from a broken heart.

'Here,' he called after him.

'What?' Laurence snapped again. Bill had never seen him look so angry.

He pulled out his wallet. Selecting a couple of £20 notes, he folded them and held them out.

'What's that for?' Laurence looked at the money contemptuously.

'Go and get yourself some paint for your room. Whatever you want.'

Laurence looked at the cash for a moment longer and then took it silently. He walked away without a word of thanks.

Bill turned to Liz, who was staring after Laurence incredulously. 'What's wrong with him? She asked.

'He must have heard us,' Bill replied. 'He *must* have. He's just trying to punish us. That's all' He paused, suddenly unsure of himself. 'Should I have shouted at him? Told him off? He shouldn't act like that to us… It was just so out-of-character. It took me aback a bit.' Another pause. 'What *is* wrong with him?'

Though Laurence had been there for barely two minutes, his visit stayed with Bill for the rest of the morning. He kept playing over the scenario in his head, dwelling on Laurence's expression – it was so unfamiliar it could almost have been another person – hearing the unrestrained anger, almost hatred in his words. It left him feeling sick and disorientated.

Everything he had done since Denise had walked out had been designed to spare Laurence any further suffering. Had he failed? The fear haunted him – it was the one thing he couldn't bear. That somehow he was responsible for any pain Laurence felt, and that through his own inadequacy he had been unable to live up to the standards of parenthood. Liz always said he was a perfectionist who tore himself apart trying to achieve every unfeasibly high aim. But when it came to Laurence's well-being, and his relationship with his son, no aim was too high.

The possibility of failure only drove him on to greater levels of determination. Wandering around the chilly, dark house, he resolved to spend more time with Laurence to try to smooth over any wrong his son felt, yet at the same time attempting to consider Liz's feelings. It would be a tough balancing act, but everything had been so good since they moved into Heol Fanog, he was not about to let the breakdown of another relationship tarnish what they had finally attained. He was prepared to fight for their happiness.

*

That afternoon, the indefatigable change in Heol Fanog, which the Riches felt on some instinctive level, started to manifest itself in a more tangible way. The mood had been building since they woke, a feeling of oppressive atmospherics, like thunder on a hot summer day, stifling and depressing. Shortly after 3 p.m. Bill was in the kitchen making a cup of coffee and Liz was in the bedroom feeding Ben. The house was still. Outside it was a bleak day; the boles of the trees black with wet, the hills above a brooding purple, the sky and fields merging into a wash of grey.

The explosion of noise startled Liz so much she involuntarily clutched Ben tightly to her breast. Her heart thumped wildly. A door further along the landing – Bill's workshop or the nursery – had slammed so loudly it sounded like it had almost burst from its hinges. Had Laurence returned in another bad mood? Or was it Bill? If Ben hadn't been suckling so peacefully she would have shouted out in anger.

Seconds later, another door slammed with ferocity, this time next door. Laurence's room. It *was* him; of course it was. When Ben had finished feeding, she would tell him what she thought of his attitude. Whatever his mood, there was no need for such a display.

And then the door of her room slammed.

Only the door didn't open or close – it was just the noise. A tremendous crashing. A piece of jewellery jumped on the dressing table. Ben pulled away from the breast and started to cry, a frightened wailing that rose and fell like a siren. Liz barely heard it. Her eyes were fixed on the door as a rush of thoughts tumbled through her mind. She had heard the door slam…

… Only it hadn't opened.

Suddenly she was trembling and she pulled Ben close, to comfort her as much as him. There was no explanation for what had happened. The unreality of it hit her like a sledgehammer and she suddenly remembered the fear she had seen in Bill's face the previous night when he had heard the footsteps.

And as that thought passed into her mind, she heard the footsteps again, crashing along the landing to her door. The breath caught in her throat as she waited for it to open.

Then Bill was there, angrily glancing around the room. 'What in heaven's name is going on?' he asked. He had heard the doors slamming from the kitchen and knowing Laurence was not in the house, he thought Liz was the culprit.

She could barely hold back the tears of anxiety as she explained what had happened, and she felt even worse as she witnessed that fear come back into Bill's face again. Neither of them was superstitious, but in that instant they realized something bizarre, inexplicable and very frightening had come into their lives.

They spent the next hour in the kitchen, talking over what had happened. After the initial shock had worn off, they tried to turn it into a joke, but the laughter was strained and neither of them was reassured. The house was haunted – short of both of them turning crazy overnight, that was the only explanation. Some people would give an arm and a leg to have a friendly ghost in the home, Bill joked. And if all it did was slam doors and run loudly along the landing in the middle of the night, well, they could live with that, couldn't they?

The presence they both felt was a different matter. Though neither of them gave voice to it, from that morning they had sensed a malevolent brooding and the constant, prickly feeling that eyes were always on them. Separately, they dismissed it as their own personal reaction to the shock of what they were discussing. Just spooking themselves. Letting their imaginations run away with them. Nothing to get worked up about. A ghost in hobnail boots – that was a fine story to tell the neighbours.

The afternoon passed in a state of heightened tension as they both tried to go about their regular duties, Bill in the studio, Liz with Ben. Laurence came in, barely paused to talk and disappeared to his room. Time seemed to be holding its breath. At 6:15 p.m., when both Bill and Liz were in the kitchen for their evening meal and talking about their ghost, the exhalation was deafening.

They both heard the footsteps at the same time. Their gaze locked on each other as all their concentration flooded into their hearing. It was upstairs once again, but this time there was a shush-shushing on the wooden floor at the top of the stairs, like the gentle tread of slippered feet.

Bill tried to keep his smile in place, but it slipped away. It was as if whatever was there had been listening to them and had decided to make its presence felt during a lull in the conversation; the punchline to a very black joke. They held their breath in the tense quiet of the house, and waited.

The footsteps fell lightly upon the top step.

Liz looked sickly pale. Outside, the winter wind had picked up in the branches of the trees. They both thought at the same time: *it's coming down*.

There was a pause, and then they heard the foot pad on the second step.

In his Moses basket, Ben stirred, kicked out; a bad dream.

The third step.

The fourth step. Pause. Fifth. Pause. Sixth.

When the steps reached the bottom, they turned and looked through the kitchen door to the hall and the foot of the stairs. There was no shadow there, no sound, but they could sense something just around the corner on the bottom step, out of sight. They waited and waited, until the tension was almost too much to bear.

Then Bill felt Liz's eyes on him, and he knew it was his responsibility. He moved forward slowly, uncomfortably, feeling like his heart was ready to burst. His own feet sounded loud on the stone flags. In the hall, he paused and then forced himself to step out to the foot of the stairs. He looked up, his mind already flashing up images of the terrors he expected.

Nothing.

His sigh was so loud it was almost a shudder. Liz saw the tautness in his face loosen and she knew that the stairs were empty. Yet there was no relief in either of them; it was no longer something they could hide with a joke. The footsteps had come at such a point that it seemed like whatever was in the house was speaking to them, and its message was very clear. *Believe.*

Liz chewed on her bottom lip as she struggled with what she felt instinctively. 'I'm frightened, Bill,' she said.

*

Bill called Swalec on Monday morning, as he had promised. It only took a moment or two for the woman on the other end to cross-check the figures on her computer and to tell him it appeared the figure of £750 was correct. It was not an estimate – the meter had been read by one of Swalec's men a few days previously. Bill calmly explained he would hardly have expected to run up that kind of bill in a year never mind a quarter; the central heating and cooker were oil-fired and they had few appliances – lamps, a fridge, a TV. The Swalec employee conceded the bill was uncommonly high compared to average use in a house the size of Heol Fanog, but she stressed the figure on the bill matched the meter reading. In anger, Bill threatened to withhold payment, and that seemed to do the trick;

she agreed to send a technician out to check for faults, but her tone implied there was little chance of finding something that could account for such a big discrepancy. When Bill replaced the phone he felt annoyed and impotent in the face of such a powerful, dehumanized entity. Yet here was something tangible that he *could* fight. He wasn't going to back down.

*

Bill spent the rest of the day completing some art for an order. He was eager to start work on his painting – the original idea was bursting into colourful life in his mind as he worked – but his responsibility was providing the income that kept the house running. There was almost an edge of desperation in his desire to begin on the clean canvas that hung in his studio. Secretly, he feared time was running away from him. It seemed to be going quicker each year. A hard core of bitterness had formed in his heart, a feeling that he had wasted all those years making what he thought had been a happy home with Denise when he could have been painting, building a body of work, creating his masterpiece. If he didn't create something soon, perhaps he never would. He couldn't bear that notion.

After an hour or two painting his intricate designs on a carved wooden chest, he decided to take a break. A little morosely, he wandered downstairs and stepped into the kitchen. The moment he crossed the threshold, he was assailed by a vile stench hanging in the air. Coughing and spluttering, he cupped his hand to his mouth and hurried back out into the hall, his eyes stung with tears.

Sulphur. He recognized the odour instantly.

Covering his mouth with his handkerchief, he stepped back into the kitchen and tried to search for the source of the smell. He checked the cooker, the heater, delved into cupboards, crawled along the floor to see if it could be seeping up from beneath. Finally he decided it must have found its way in from the cesspit in the garden. Heol Fanog was so isolated it wasn't on a sewer system, yet they regularly had the cesspit checked and they hadn't found a problem with it before. He couldn't really understand how it could cause such a sulphurous stench in the kitchen, but that was a job for the experts.

He went into the hall and phoned a company to check the system and when he returned to the kitchen the smell had gone. There wasn't even an after-trace in the air.

*

A couple of men came to test the cesspit an hour later. They looked at Bill strangely when he described the sulphurous smell and told them how quickly it had vanished. After carrying out several checks for a quarter of an hour, they couldn't find anything wrong, but they told Bill to call them again if the smell came back.

*

That night, when Ben was asleep and Laurence was upstairs in his room, Liz came in to Bill who was reading in the lounge.

'There's another smell,' she said in a curious tone.

'Not again,' he said wearily. He tossed his book on the sofa. 'Is it really disgusting?'

She shook her head. Taking him by the hand, she led him through the kitchen and into the hall. 'There. Can you smell it?'

Bill sniffed the air, tensing in the anticipation of the acrid burn on his throat. Instead a sickly-sweet aroma with a touch of spice assailed him. It ignited a nagging recognition in his mind, but he couldn't quite place it. 'What is it?'

'Incense.'

'Incense?' He looked at Liz as if to ask her what she was doing burning incense.

'It's nothing to do with me,' she said. 'I was just passing through and smelled it.'

‘It’s got to come from somewhere,’ Bill said with a brusqueness borne of uncertainty. He glanced around the darkened hall, at the closed door, which led into the barn, through the window into the dark, moonless night. The trees around the house were thrashing in the wind; a storm was building.

‘I read a story once,’ Liz said quietly. Bill shook his head; he didn’t want to hear. ‘About a haunting. Just before the ghost appeared the air would be filled with the powerful scent of perfume. Those footsteps, Bill. And that stink this afternoon, and now this…’ She didn’t have to say any more.

Bill led her back into the light of the kitchen. ‘There’s no need to be scared,’ he said. ‘So there are a few odd sounds and strange smells. This is a chance to approach a great mystery. We can fire our curiosity and investigate it first hand.’ He tried to be upbeat, but there, so far away from humanity and with the wild night crashing around the house, it was difficult.

‘It’s more than that,’ Liz said, moving closer to him until they were hugging each other. ‘If it was just sounds and smells I could cope with it. But it’s that feeling that someone’s watching us. That there’s always someone standing in the corner of the room, or just outside the door, waiting… waiting until we get close…’

That constant sensation of an invisible presence got to him too. It wasn’t simply feeling there was someone else in the room; it was the fact that it seemed evil. That it wanted to hurt him.

The storm broke, and against the distant bang of thunder, he heard drops of rain start to pound against the window. Suddenly it felt like they were in the loneliest place on earth.

*

The smells came and went over the next few days, sometimes sulphur, sometimes incense, but gradually another anomaly made its presence felt. Liz was the first to recognize it, as she fed Ben in the kitchen one day. It was a bitter cold morning with a sharp hoar frost glittering on the ground in the sunlight.

For the past few days she had been nagging Bill to turn up the heating. That morning he finally seemed to have complied, although a little too enthusiastically. Liz was sweltering. As Ben suckled, sweat trickled between her breasts and plastered her hair to her forehead. The kitchen was as hot as a foundry.

When Ben had finished feeding she called out to Bill who was tinkering with the car outside. The battery seemed to have gone flat overnight and he was desperately trying to find the source of the fault. Bill discovered the problem first thing when he went to move the car away from the house so there was room to put some of his samples in the boot. When he came in wiping his hands on a rag, Liz said, 'Turn the heating down, will you, love. It's like an inferno in here.'

He started to say, 'It's not on,' but then he felt the wave of heat as he stepped into the kitchen. Curiously, he checked the gauge on the boiler – the needle was on zero – and then he placed a hand on the radiator.

'Cold,' he said. 'I forgot to put the heating on this morning because I was so wrapped up about the car.'

And then the recognition dawned on her, and Bill a split-second later. Another sign. One more pointer that their world was keeling off-balance and about to go spinning out of control.

They felt that with each new shock a door was opening a little wider, allowing another sensation from a strange and terrifying world to creep through. First sound, then smell, and now feeling.

The next day, Bill experienced a cold spot in the hall. So chill it felt like a bucket of ice water down his spine, yet the rest of the house was warm from the central heating. It faded soon after without any explanation. The hot and cold spots materialized without any rhyme or reason across the ground floor of the house. When Bill or Liz stepped into them unexpectedly, it was like the fingers of the unknown were touching their nerves.

Bill still thought of it as a puzzle, but with each day it was starting to lose a little bit more of any intellectual appeal it had held when it had first begun. Instead, he felt something overcome him, which was much older and deeper than rational thought. Coupled with it was a sense of apprehension: what was going to happen *next*?

Bill's testimony: 'Nobody heard the footsteps on the first occasion, when I did, and I want to impress upon you what my state of mind was. I suppose I was quite fortunate that that was the first experience I'd ever had of something like that. And it happened at such a late hour that I was ready to go to sleep anyway. So when you wake up in the morning, you think, Wow! Could it really happen anyway? And you go on.

'Shortly after, though, there was this veil effect coming down and it all happened at once… the strange smells starting to appear downstairs. Liz became aware of the footsteps. They started to happen daily, at around the usual time, which wasn't the time I heard them, but about 6.15 p.m. Boots, heavy. Then, intermingling with that, there would be soft footsteps coming down the stairs – this was a slippered foot. I still don't know what Laurence heard because he's very embarrassed about it all.

'When the first smells came, they smelt of incense and sulphur, which is quite strange. I know what incense smells like from going into Catholic church and that sort of thing. And the other smell, well, that was a devilish sort of smell. I realize that we had a septic tank, but it had been cleaned out some weeks before by a Hereford firm called Green Apple, and the drainage going to it had been cleaned out as well, so we knew it couldn't be from the drains. These smells came at the same time as the temperature changes. They'd be in the area by the telephone, the hallway, always concentrated by that area. The temperature changes would happen in that place as well as the kitchen. You could find yourself in a hot situation or a very, very cold one.

'Your mind would tell you at the same time that there was something looking at you, there was something breathing over your shoulder. On your face. One could feel the wind. All times of the day. There was this 6.15 thing that was fairly regular, but as far as the temperature changes happened, we could go for days without anything happening, but there could be three in a day. But we were aware that something was happening.'

*

Early one morning Bill walked the dog along the lanes for more than an hour to be alone with his thoughts. On his way back he encountered one of his neighbours, who was leaning on a fence looking out over the fields. Bill knew the man by sight, but not by name. They exchanged a few pleasantries and then began to chat. The man seemed strangely interested in how Bill and his family were settling in to Heol Fanog.

At first Bill was loath to discuss the strange events of the previous few days – in daylight it seemed too ridiculous to discuss with a stranger – but they were so much on Bill's mind that gradually they emerged. To Bill's surprise the man didn't seem in the slightest daunted at the mention of the footsteps, temperature changes and the smells. Bill got the sense this wasn't the first time his neighbour had heard of those things.

'Has it happened before?' he asked eagerly. He wanted to know he and Liz weren't alone in their experiences. If others had been through it, then they weren't imagining it. More, they weren't *causing* it.

To Bill's disappointment, the neighbour simply looked away towards the hills. Then he said, cryptically, 'There is no good luck there.'

Bill asked him what he meant, but he would only say previous residents 'had not had the best of times' at Heol Fanog. Abstractly, he asked Bill what he thought of the old manor house in the grounds.

'Why?' Bill said curiously.

'No reason' the man replied, but he knew he couldn't leave it at that. 'It's just that the Gandys… just up the way… they used some material from the old manor for some building work a while back. When it was delivered, you know what they found? Gravestones.

There was a whole load of them which had been leaning against part of the ruins.'

'Where did they come from?' Bill asked. He felt a strange tingling in his fingertips.

'Well, these big old houses, they often had their own private burial plot, you know? When they died, the family members used to get buried within shouting distance of the house. Maybe that's what there is there. It's so overgrown now you'd never know, but there's no other reasons for the gravestones to be there.' And then he added, 'You don't know if any of those gravestones were used in the conversion of your place do you?'

'They used some material from the ruins,' Bill replied. 'But there's no sign of gravestones.'

'But you can't say they didn't, can you?' the neighbour continued.

'No,' Bill said. 'I can't.'

The neighbour smiled politely and strode away without another word.

*

Laurence returned from town by taxi with a large cardboard box filled with two big cans of paint and a brush. Bill cheerily asked to see what he had bought, but Laurence stalked past him up the stairs and slammed the door of his room.

Armed with a couple of boxes of his own, Bill followed Laurence up a few minutes later and knocked on the door. It took two more knocks before his son relented and let him in. Laurence swung the door open and returned to his bed where he lay with his hands behind his head, as if Bill wasn't there.

'You've got the paint, I see,' Bill ventured.

No reply.

‘Do you want any help with the decoration. I can spare –‘

‘I’ll do it myself.’

‘OK. Well, don’t knock yourself out.’ He walked in and placed the boxes he was carrying on the floor. ‘I’ve bought you a present.’

Laurence eyed the boxes suspiciously and then continued to stare at the ceiling. ‘I’ll open them later.’

Bill waited uncomfortably for a second or two in case there was any other response, and then he slipped out quietly. Laurence had never kept one of his moods going for so long before. It was much worse than a simple reaction to his and Liz’s love-making; Bill sensed a sea change in his son on some level he couldn’t quite understand. It was almost like he was dealing with a different person. He wondered if he should confront him about it so they could sit and talk it out, or if it would be better to let Laurence deal with whatever was going through his head himself and hope it would blow itself out. He was desperately afraid of doing the wrong thing; more, of losing his son.

Downstairs, Liz asked him how Laurence had liked his present, a portable TV and video for his bedroom, which Bill had bought in Brecon that day. It was part peace offering, part an attempt to allow Laurence some space of his own in the household. Bill tried to find the words, but he was too troubled to talk about it.

Laurence started work on his room that night. Bill and Liz heard the sound of paint being slapped around through the walls, and the disturbance carried on long past midnight.

Let him do what he wants, Bill thought as he tried to get to sleep. Carping at him all the time will only make him feel worse.

In fact, Bill thought the painting might be therapeutic and allow Laurence to work out some of his problems. He’ll be better in the morning, Bill thought as he finally drifted off.

At breakfast Bill asked Laurence how the painting had gone. His son looked exhausted, but at least it kept the anger from his face.

Suddenly, Laurence said he had finished, but he refused to take Bill upstairs to show him his handiwork. After Bill and Liz had taken him to the bus for school, they went up to check for themselves, laughing together as they sneaked along the landing before throwing open the door.

All playfulness caught instantly in their throat. They were met with a sight that was both shocking and threatening.

Laurence had painted the entire room red. It was a deep shade, the colour of blood, and it was so oppressive in its intensity it made them feel heady.

'Oh Lord, is this how he feels?' Bill said quietly.

Standing in the centre of the room, all he could sense was anger, radiating out of every wall, a brooding, powerful force that threatened to sweep them away.

'How can he bear to sleep in here?' Liz asked.

Bill sighed. 'Well, it's his room. He does what he wants. If he wants bad dreams, that's what he'll get.'

Slowly they trailed out, all lightheartedness drained from them. 'This place is getting to him,' Bill added quietly.

When Liz returned from taking Ben for a walk, Bill stormed up to her before she had got the pram through the gate. It was a grey, drizzling afternoon and Bill was only wearing his shirtsleeves, but in his anger he seemed oblivious to the rain. Liz steeled herself to hear Laurence had committed some new outrage.

'They've cancelled,' Bill snapped.

'Who?'

'Those people who gave me that big order last month.'

'The West Country –'

'Yes, the West Country people.'

‘But they were so interested. They loved your work, Bill. They were raving about it so much I thought you could have charged double. What could possibly have gone wrong?’

Bill shook his head, suddenly deflated. ‘I don’t know. They just rang up and said they couldn’t take the order. No reason. It was as simple as that.’

Liz paused and then said, ‘But we were counting on that money.’

Bill nodded. ‘I know.’

‘Well, what are we going to do now?’

‘Something will come up. It always does. And we’ve got that other order. It’s smaller, I know, but with a bit of belt-tightening it could tide us over until something else comes in.’

Later that afternoon, the other order was cancelled at short notice. ‘I tried to find out the reason, but they couldn’t give me an answer. They were so vague… like they didn’t even know themselves.’ It was the first time it had happened to Bill in all his years of working.

*

As twilight fell, Bill and Liz had to get out of the house. Everything that they had planned for in the relaxed days of summer was falling apart. They both felt shell-shocked, not just from the order cancellations, but from the tensions caused by Laurence’s mood, and most of all from the fear that there was some presence in the house with them. Bill remembers feeling like a single soldier trying to hold a hill against an army advancing on all sides.

The rain pounded into them on the back of the razored wind that drove down from the hills. Yet as they meandered along the deserted lanes, discussing what had happened to them and what they could do, they felt a strange sensation, which hit them both at the same time. The grim claustrophobia of Heol Fanog lifted, as if they had walked through a curtain into another place. It was such a tangible sensation they both looked at each other questioningly.

‘You felt it too,’ Liz said after a second. Bill nodded. She thought for a moment and then added, ‘Remember when we came here we felt Heol Fanog was surrounded by this wonderful protective dome, where inside it was warm and golden and we were safe from the world? Well, now it feels like it’s turned inside out. Around the house I feel trapped and under attack. Out here I suddenly feel free, like we’ve escaped. Like we’ve gone beyond its reach.’

Bill looked back up the lane and across the fields to the cluster of black trees where Heol Fanog lay. The gloom was starting to fall. ‘We can’t stay out here forever,’ he muttered.

‘I’m afraid to go back,’ Liz said. And then after a long pause, ‘I’m afraid it’s going to get worse.’

Chapter 3

As 1989 slipped into 1990, the most palpable change in Heol Fanog was the sweeping sense of disbelief that engulfed Bill and Liz. It was as if they had been involved in some terrible accident, and they couldn't understand why it was happening to them. Nor could they grasp the mechanics of a situation that had turned a happy life into an unhappy one virtually overnight. Sometimes in those dark days of winter, when the snow lay so thick in the lanes they were prisoners in the house, they would sit and watch the video they had made of the family during the previous summer, trying to work out what had gone wrong, how so many things could come crashing down at once.

The haunting had forced them to reassess not only their lives, but also *life*, and it had shaken their grasp of mundane reality. Suddenly they were in a hall of distorting mirrors where once innocuous events loomed large and mishaps were transformed into disasters. It was not all in their mind, though; they were sure of that. They felt victimized, but their adversary was not apparent. That added an unreal aspect to their existence, as if things were being shifted behind the scenery of their lives and they only saw the results days later. It became a case of if something could go wrong, it would go wrong; so many problems, failures, disappointments, that they started to see an intelligence behind the random bad luck. That was a dangerous path, they knew, but they couldn't help their gut response. Who's out to get us? they joked. And what have we ever done to harm anybody? But the downward spiral continued, nevertheless.

In a matter of weeks, they had problems with every animal in the house. Lulu the goat gave birth to two kids and then accidentally crushed one of them. Bill's pet Rigland picked up a disease and had to be shot. The dog Bill had bought for Laurence after Denise left went mad and ran away. Laurence's guinea pig, Henry, died. And Sheena, one of the family cats, also went mad, running crazily around in circles in the house. Liz couldn't bear to have it put down so her mother agreed to care for it.

The dispute with the electricity company dragged on inexorably. After Bill had refused to pay the initial invoice the family seemed to have become trapped in a labyrinth of correspondence, claim and counter-claim. They felt powerless trying to convince a faceless, inflexible authority that they were not seeking to evade payment.

In a matter of months, Bill's business had gone from booming to the verge of extinction. Orders that in the past had been set in stone were suddenly cancelled. Rich buyers from New York and Los Angeles raved about his samples, promising to buy thousands of pounds worth of work, yet when Bill phoned them up later they had mysteriously lost interest; more than that, they had almost forgotten they had seen his art. Samples vanished *en route* to interested parties.

Examining the situation rationally, that period was not a good time for any business. The post-housing boom recession was biting hard. Businesses were failing across the land and Bill's – basically a luxury service – was certainly in line for hardship as a non-essential when it came to cost-cutting. But even that did not explain the speed and severity of the collapse; Bill's bank manager and accountant were stunned by how quickly everything fell apart.

To put it into perspective, it is important to understand his previous success. He had received worldwide acclaim – an agent took two of his major works to California for an exhibition in Beverly Hills, backed by a prominent arts magazine. The movie actor Sylvester Stallone, who collects modern art, and a host of other Hollywood glitterati were expected to attend with chequebooks at the ready. Yet shortly after those November footsteps and only days before the exhibition, the agency went bust. Bill's paintings were left to languish in a vault while creditors wrangled over who actually owned them, an argument expected to continue for years.

The testament to his previous success is apparent everywhere. His paintings have been bought by Matthew Pritchard, chairman of the Welsh Arts Council, and the Countess of Westmorland, while George Melly, the performer and an acclaimed critic of surreal painting, highly praised his work.

Naturally, Bill's business problems bought money worries. Although the rent on Heol Fanog was only around £50 a week, the Riches had enjoyed a good lifestyle during 1989 and they had to cut back. The Volvo was sold and they purchased a workday second-hand car. Luxuries were pruned to the bone; the only thing not restricted was food for Ben and Laurence. They seemed to be trapped in a spiral of deprivation, with a new crisis coming after each cutback to force further cutbacks. The cars were a particular worry. Whenever they were parked outside the front of the house, the batteries seemed to drain overnight and electrical faults developed with increasing regularity to the point where many problems could not be rectified and a new car had to be bought. It was a hard time, but Bill and Liz were resolute in their optimism. The good time hadn't been so long ago; they would be back soon.

Laurence, however, was an increasing worry for both of them. He was unrecognizable as the happy, outgoing boy who had moved into Heol Fanog in May 1989, a complete transformation had happened in days. All his spare time in the house was spent in his blood-red room behind a locked door. The video and TV Bill had installed in the bedroom as a gift for his son were used to watch an array of increasingly grotesque horror films, which seemed to have become an obsession. During the night Bill and Liz could hear the screams through their bedroom wall.

Whenever Laurence encountered his father and stepmother, over the occasional meal he didn't eat in his room, or passing on the way to the toilet or out of the house, he would treat them with complete contempt. Rage burned inside him, one that occasionally erupted in shouted abuse and veiled threats. Seeing what had happened to his son tore Bill apart. He tried everything to rebuild his relationship with Laurence; ignoring his outbursts, bringing him a cooked breakfast in bed every Sunday, answering his every need, offering to go on trips with him. Liz wasn't so forgiving. She blamed Laurence for some of the pressures that were starting to manifest in the house, although she still treated him civilly.

Again, rationally, Laurence's transformation *could* be attributed to the change through which all teenagers go. How many parents think their child has suddenly turned into a monster? And then there were the psychological scars that Laurence undoubtedly inherited from the break-up of his parents' marriage. He was aware of his mother's affair when he had barely broken into his teens, long before she walked out on Bill. And he had seen his mother replaced in the family home by a younger, more attractive woman, one he didn't even slightly know. Any psychiatrist will explain the deep effect of these things on a young mind.

Yet, once more, it is impossible to ignore the speed of the change. Before Bill heard the footsteps that cold night in November 1989, Laurence was a pleasant, open teenager, albeit one who suffered occasional bouts of sulkiness and irritation. Soon after he had developed an anger, contempt and hatred, which had never been evident before. In a matter of hours he walled himself off from those who loved him and started a seething war of attrition. It was too much, but even those outside the household could claim his change was just within the bounds of possibility. Soon it got worse.

And against all this was the haunting, continuing relentlessly. Bill and Liz gradually had to come to terms with the belief that their home was not their own – they shared it with something else. The footsteps manifested repeatedly. Bill could be working in his studio or cooking a meal, or Liz could be playing with Ben, and there would come the sudden sound of boots pounding along the landing. On other occasions there were the soft shufflings of the slippers down the stairs. Tangible things, not imagination, but never anyone there. After the initial shock would come a feeling of dread so strong it made them want to flee the house, and what made it worse was that even if they ran away there was nowhere for them to go; they would have to return sooner or later.

How hard to believe that such a simple thing as the sound of a footstep could have a tremendous effect on someone's life. For Bill and Liz, it made them reappraise their whole existence. One can half-believe in the supernatural in a detached way, yet when confronted with seeming evidence on a daily basis the Riches felt they had no choice but to believe. Immersed in that reality no other explanation came anywhere close to making sense to them. They found themselves considering what might be beyond death, what could lurk around you constantly, unseen but able to affect you. It is a small step psychologically, but a terrible one because once that boundary of rationality has been crossed, there is a nightmarish world where anything can happen. When the props that hold up life fall down, the unknown and unknowable sweeps in and suddenly the only emotion one can comprehend is fear. That psychological instability haunted Bill and Liz as much as the unseen spirits.

They wondered constantly what was in the house with them, moving closer, what it could do to them when it decided the time was right. They prayed it would leave them alone so they could get on with their lives.

The foul smells also repeatedly manifested, like a tweak on the hairs at the nape of the neck whenever their minds wandered from the fear: the odour of sulphur, so vile it made them hack, appearing from nowhere then disappearing minutes later; the cloying, sickly aroma of incense drifting across the hall and into the kitchen. The temperature changes, too, added to the air of unreality which pervaded Heol Fanog. Sometimes the kitchen or the hall would become baking hot, enough to make them flushed and sweaty, yet there was snow on the ground outside and the central heating was switched off. Then a room would be plunged into such arctic cold that in an instant their teeth would start to chatter and their fingers would turn blue.

One of the worst things could not be so easily defined. It was a feeling, a sixth sense, that set the hairs on their arms prickling. Sometimes, in the kitchen, they would both look round at exactly the same moment and then glance at each other knowingly, a shared sensation that could not be put down to imagination. And with that constant feeling of being watched was the certain knowledge that the watcher was evil. There were times when they stood at the top of the stairs sure that someone wanted to push them down. The malignant presence never left them alone.

Their options were limited. Their worsening financial situation precluded them from buying a property, and the chances of renting a family-sized house were slim; most landlords in the area charged tourist rates of up to £500 a week. Any decently priced rented property that did come on the market was immediately over-subscribed. Coupled with this was the fact that Bill was not the kind of man who would turn tail and run, even when things were at their blackest; his home was his castle and he refused to be driven from it.

The inexplicable events happened with such regularity they became an everyday part of Bill and Liz's life. Each time something happened it would turn the screw a little bit more, increasing their anxiety until the stress was at such a level they felt like soldiers on the frontline, waiting for an order to go over the top.

*

Bill's testimony: 'With Laurence, it was quite strange, I remember thinking at the time. He should have started badly and gradually got better, because he would have become used to the new situation with the stepmother and used to the new routine. It all started so wonderfully until the footsteps, and then he became a very obnoxious teenager. Before that he still had to have his own private little wars with Liz. I can remember when we were walking around a museum in Cairo, all having diarrhoea and all searching for a loo at the same time, and he was wandering up behind Liz and putting two fingers up. But that I can put down to simple age problems. He started to change about the time of the footsteps. And when I say change I mean that there was such a difference to his character and temperament, it was beyond anybody's understanding. Normally he was a placid, quiet, normal kid – not into glue-sniffing, or dope or anything like that. But after that… There was something out to destroy him. I know that now more than ever before. It was not as if he was the easiest target and… yes, he was possessed.

'He didn't go to a local school; he stayed in the one in the village where we were living before we moved to Brecon. It was about six miles away, so I was taking him every day. There was no bus service. I used to take him there alone and Liz used to come with me to pick him up, and he was always in a foul temper, a foul mood. It wasn't him at all.

'It got so bad at that time, when all the other phenomena were building up, that Liz was getting very pissed off with him – not just his behaviour, but with everything else. It was happening when the *big* whirl was going on, round about December 1989, January 1990. Nobody could quite understand what was happening: it was turmoil, like we were on a boat in the middle of the sea and we just had to wait for the wind to drop to understand exactly if we were going to sink or where we were going to end up, washed up or whatever.'

*

There were other strange things happening beyond the main phenomena. One morning when Bill and Liz were downstairs, they heard the sound of the piano in Bill's studio. Notes were picked out carefully, echoing throughout the house. They looked at each other in terror and then drove themselves upstairs to investigate. As they reached the door, the music stopped.

Nervously, they stepped inside. The room was empty apart from a cat curled up in a chair on the other side of the room.

Bill forced a smile before closing the door hurriedly. 'Just the cat. That's a relief.'

But neither of them believed it.

*

In the New Year, a pleading call convinced Bill's mother to visit. Bill and Liz felt they needed someone from outside the house to give them some perspective on the strange events, and his mother seemed the perfect choice; her no-nonsense, down-to-earth approach to life was the perfect counterpoint to the sense of unreality that pervaded Heol Fanog. Mrs Rich found it hard to believe the incredible things Bill and Liz told her, but she sensed the pressures in the household and agreed to stay for a weekend.

Whatever force was inhabiting Heol Fanog retreated, but it didn't go away completely. On the Saturday afternoon, Liz and Mrs Rich were downstairs when the footsteps pounded along the upstairs landing. It seemed to be an act of defiance in the face of Mrs Rich's scepticism, but although she heard she wouldn't discuss it.

That evening Mrs Rich was still waiting to see her grandson: Laurence had been avoiding her since her arrival. In a way, Bill was almost relieved. The changes in Laurence seemed to have increased rapidly in the days leading up to his grandmother's visit. No good or kind words came from his anymore; there was only abuse and anger. Most disturbing for Bill was how Laurence's face seemed to be changing. It seemed to Bill that there was not a trace of innocence any more; the cheeks had drawn in, the eyes grown hollow, the brow furrowed. His mouth shifted between a sneer and a snarl and his eyes radiated a permanent blazing fury. Sometimes it almost seemed like his physical characteristics were altering, as if he was starting to look like a different person. It frightened Bill on a very basic level, and for the first time he wondered what if the cause of that transformation might lie in what was happening in Heol Fanog. The thought scared him too much to consider it in any deep way.

At 7.30 p.m., Bill, Liz and Mrs Rich were sitting in the lounge when they heard the familiar clumping sounds of Laurence coming downstairs.

'I think it's about time I had a word with him, don't you?' Mrs Rich said with a smile.

Bill wanted to caution her, but it was too late – she was already up and out. Bill and Liz followed quickly behind as Mrs Rich called to Laurence and asked him to wait. When they made it into the kitchen they saw Laurence had paused at the foot of the stairs and was glowering as Mrs Rich approached.

'Laurence –' she began.

'Get away from me.' Bill and Liz froze. It didn't sound like Laurence's voice. It was guttural, filled with hatred, almost an old man's voice.

Mrs Rich looked like she had been slapped in the face. 'Laurence...' she said again, almost pleading this time.

‘Fuck off!’ he raged. Then he leaned forward and, according to Bill, spat in her face.

Her cry of shock and subsequent tears were lost as Bill burst by her, raging. Laurence stormed up the stairs and the paused midway and turned as Bill reached the foot.

‘Laurence! Get down here! Apologize to you grandmother! I don’t know what’s. _’

‘Fuck off,’ Laurence snapped again. And for the merest instant Bill saw through him, saw that it wasn’t Laurence, that someone else was behind his face, in his face, much older and incalculably evil. A gobbet of saliva burst from his mouth and hit Bill in the eye. While Bill was wiping it away in shock, Laurence pounded up the stairs and slammed his bedroom door behind him, drawing the bolt with a thunderous finality.

Bill, Liz and Mrs Rich drifted into the lounge in a state of disbelief. Laurence’s actions were the natural culmination of what had been happening since the night of the footsteps in November 1989, yet it was still unbelievable that it had come so far, so quickly.

After the tears had subsided, Bill agonized over whether he had done the right thing. Should he have been more forceful? He had always believed abuse would only escalate a situation, but he knew from what he had seen in Laurence’s face that he couldn’t reason with him either. What could he do? He felt feeble, like he had lost control of his life. He felt like he had lost his son.

When Mrs Rich had gone to bed, Liz said to Bill, ‘Did you see where it happened?’ He looked puzzled. ‘In the hall. Everything that’s been happening has been going on around there. In the kitchen, the stairs, the landing and Laurence’s room above. The hall is the centre of it all.’

Bill thought about her words for a moment and then said, ‘This is out of control. I’m terrified, for us, for Laurence. God, I love him. I want to save him. What are we going to do?’

Liz thought for a moment and then said quietly, 'I think we need help.'

*

That night Liz and Bill were woken by a terrible howling from Laurence's room. In that awful sound there was pain and rage and at times it didn't sound human. Bill hammered on the door, but the howling didn't stop, and when he tried the handle it was locked. He considered breaking it down, but feared it would only make the situation worse.

After ten minutes, Laurence's raging stopped and was punctuated by two loud crashes, then a low, pitiful whimpering which drifted into an uneasy silence that was almost as awful.

In the morning, after Laurence had left the house, Bill and Liz went into his room. Over his bed two holes had been punched in the plasterboard fascia that covered the stone walls. They could see the mark of his knuckles where he had rammed with all his strength. In the incarnadine glow from the walls, the room seemed to seethe angrily; clothes and videos were strewn everywhere. It looked as if he had lost himself to a wild, uncontrollable rage.

*

Bill's testimony: 'That was the one confrontation that stuck in my mind, and there were many of them, but it was because my mother was there, Liz was there, and we'd just experienced four, maybe five, episodes of the phenomena at the one time that Laurence really broke the back of the camel. When he told me to fuck off and spat in my face, well, I don't know quite what had put him in that state of mind. I know it wasn't anything I had said to him or anybody else had said to him. I can put my mind back to that moment because it's like it's on a video camera – I thought how I'd brought this kid up and how I used to smack his bum sometimes when he needed it, and I thought, What do I do now, when he's even larger than me? I could maybe say, "You're upsetting me," but that wouldn't be acceptable to him either. What did he look like? Hatred. Hatred would be the word, and that upset me more than anything else because I didn't want him to look at me like that. He was despising me – it was horrible.'

*

Bill needed time to himself to decide what to do. There had to be a solution, but it was as if every time he came close to discovering it, it slipped back into the strange fog that had filled his mind for the last few weeks. Somewhere deep inside his head a voice was screaming: *Get out of here. Get as far away as possible*, but it was always subdued by another voice, one he didn't recognize. Calming, seductive. *Stay. Things will get easier. Don't think about it.*

The birdsong started up in the back garden in earnest, but it was a strange cacophony he had never heard before. The more he strained, the more the birds' cries sounded like human voices. *We need yoooou. We need yoooou.* With a shudder, he hurried upstairs.

Slipping into his workroom, he decided to utilize the time by starting work on his painting. There were no orders piling up, nothing to do but brood about Laurence, and sometime answers came to him when he was lost in the powerful flow of his creative energy.

The picture was coming together clearly in his mind. Oddly, it seemed to be taking shape while he slept, sweeping through his subconscious to lie in increasingly glorious colour and definition when he opened his eyes to the day. It was going to be a big piece of work, and complex, and Bill knew that to get it exactly how he envisioned it would take a lot of planning. On a large sheet of white paper he drew a grid. He would rough-out the picture on it, and then do detailed sketches of each square of the grid before he started painting.

As his pencil skimmed across the paper he felt a *frisson* of excitement coupled with a sensation so unique and rare that he wanted to hold on to it forever; that feeling, of creating something from nothing was the ultimate high, yet elusive as any drug trip.

Downstairs, Liz was coping by immersing herself in complete devotion to Ben. By focusing on her child, his innocence, his needs, she could blot everything else out; it simply wasn't happening. Ben was all.

When he finally fell asleep, there was no distraction, and her thought drifted back to her conversation with Bill in bed the previous night. They had discussed the possibility that they were going crazy, a joint psychosis like some virus passing back and forth between them. Heol Fanog was a cauldron of anxiety, and for all of them there was no escape. Surely all those pressures would have an effect on their psychological state. Yes, Laurence had heard the footsteps, and Bill's mother too. But did they just believe because Bill and Liz had pleaded their case so forcefully? Were they imagining everything else – the sounds, the smells, the temperature changes? Taking a series of coincidences, daydreams and imaginings and turning them into an explanation for their own misfortune? They were well aware that the human mind couldn't cope easily with the simple reality that bad things happened to good people for no reason, and it was eminently possible that they were searching so hard for an explanation as to why their happy life had deteriorated that they had found one, however bizarre. It had eventually turned into a ridiculous chicken-and-egg conversation: was there an evil presence in the house systematically destroying their lives, or had they imagined the presence to explain the destruction?

'I can't believe this is happening to us,' Bill said after a while. 'What have we done to deserve all this?'

'We haven't done anything,' Liz replied. 'That's the frightening thing. That you can find yourself in this situation… that you can suffer… for no reason.' She chewed on her nail as she stared into the middle distance. 'I'm scared, Bill. Terrified. I feel there's something following me just a few steps behind and I have this awful feeling that it wants to hurt me. When I'm away from the house, shopping in Brecon or something, I can put it all down to imagination. But here… I *know* there's something here. Sometimes you just know things like that, don't you?'

'We could move away.'

‘But where would be go, Bill? Realistically, where could we go? You know how much trouble we had finding Heol Fanog. Round here, there’s always a queue a mile long for any property up for rent. We can’t afford to buy with our money situation. We could try and get on the housing list, but God knows how long it would be before we became a priority.’

‘There’s our parents…’

‘Can you imagine living with either of them with Ben and Laurence for any period of time. It would drive us all mad.’

‘And this isn’t driving us mad?’

Liz ignored him. ‘I want to know who it is, Bill. If we could discover who was haunting the place we might be able to find out *why* they’re haunting it. We might finally understand why we’re suffering.’

‘And if we discovered that we might be able to stop it. You know, lay the spirit to rest like they do in all the movies.’

‘It’s so unreal. This *feels* like a movie. I never dreamed I would ever experience something like this. If someone had told me you’re going to have a ghost in your house, I would have laughed in their face.’ She took a deep breath and brought out the thought that had been eating away at her for so long. ‘It’s the feeling that it’s something evil that gets to me the most. A nice, quiet woman in white I could cope with, but it seems such a threatening presence. Sometimes I’m afraid of what’s going to happen to us.’

Liz looked to Bill for reassurance, but he couldn’t give it; he felt the same. ‘Perhaps whoever is haunting the place did something wicked in their life. This is the punishment, and they’re holding a grudge for their suffering. That’s how it often goes.’

‘Is it? Who laid down the rules for this?’

‘Well, it’s a commonly held belief from people who’ve been through these things before.’

Liz shook her head. 'When you get into this area, there aren't any rules... that's the terrifying thing. You can't count on anything.'

Bill laughed. 'We're talking about it like it's definitely real. We could still be fooling each other, you know. All the worries and the pressures could have made us particularly susceptible. Maybe if we took a step back... I mean, who would believe us if we told them?'

'I've been thinking about that. What happens if this sort of thing goes on all the time? *All* the time, Bill. We wouldn't want to talk about it in the newsagent's or the greengrocer's in case people thought we were touched. That means other people wouldn't want to make it common knowledge either, so they'd suffer in silence just like us. Imagine what that could mean. In villages and towns right across the country, right across the world, people could be facing up to awful supernatural experiences, and in the morning they go out and smile at their neighbour to save face. So no one's ever the wiser. This could be *normal*, Bill, God help us.'

'That sort of thing would get out –'

'You mean newspapers would write about it seriously instead of treating it like a joke when someone rings up to tell them. You think scientists would investigate it when doctors can't even take herbalism seriously – the things we have seen *work* on our own son? Perhaps it's happening all over, Bill, and perhaps that's how it likes it, in the dark, secretly, so it can carry on attacking people without respite –'

Bill laughed. 'You'll be saying it's the devil next.'

Liz stared through into the darkened hall. 'I don't know what it is, Bill.'

*

To Liz, the prospect that it could all be in their heads was almost more terrifying. A little madness becoming a big madness, until it showed them up to be little more frightened than children. She had to know if her view of herself as a psychologically robust individual was wrong. She *had* to know.

She ransacked a drawer in the lounge to find the house rental papers and the phone number of the landlord. A well-to-do member of Brecon society, Phil Holbourn was detached and not always approachable. Liz was afraid she wouldn't be able to contact him, but he answered the phone first time and after a minute or two away from the receiver he managed to locate the information she desired; the new phone number of Heol Fanog's previous resident. Before he hung up, Liz asked him if he had heard of anything supernatural happening in Heol Fanog. She knew his own mother had lived in the house for many years shortly after it had been converted.

'No, nothing at all like that,' he replied. 'Why do you ask?'

Liz bit her lip and wondered if she dared tell him. In the end, the words just tumbled out. 'Because I think we've got a ghost.'

Surprisingly, Holbourn didn't laugh at her. 'No, I've never heard of anything unusual,' he repeated.

Scrawling the number on the wall above the phone, Liz replaced the receiver and stared at it for a moment. She was almost afraid to dial. If she was told nothing strange had happened in Heol Fanog before, she would have to face the fact that the fear was of their own making. All in their heads. Crazy, weak people.

Nervously, she began to punch out the number.

*

The testimony of Bridget Buscombe, former resident of Heol Fanog: 'I loved the house and felt very happy there. I used to live in an isolated farmhouse in Cornwall. I spent a lot of time on my own there because my husband was a vet with the Ministry of Agriculture and he was often out. That house always had a cold, uncomfortable feeling and an eerie presence – I loathed being there on my own. But I never felt that about Heol Fanog, and I lived there for seven years. I left there reluctantly and it's always been my favourite house of all the ones I've lived in. If I had the money, I'd buy it. There was a big garden and it was overgrown when we moved there, but we cleared it and made it look nice. It was beautiful – I'd never been anywhere with so many birds, always singing. We never had any problems with the electricity bill. It was always low, you know, normal.

'I often used to go and sit in the ruins and read because it seemed really friendly down there. I used to work full-time so I'd do nutty things like hanging out my washing at midnight, but I never felt anything strange. Some people did get spooked there, I know. It was draughty and a wind would blow up around the house – houses of that age do creak and groan and moan.

'Having said that, something did happen to me which I couldn't explain. It was when I was lying in bed one night and there was no one else in the house. I was reading and I suddenly heard a noise so I looked up. I had an old spinning-wheel in one corner and the wheel was going round. Just going round of its own accord. I jumped out of bed and stuffed a piece of paper in the wheel to stop it. Why did it happen? I couldn't explain it. But I firmly believe that if you want to see something, you do, and if you don't, you don't. And I didn't want to see anything.'

*

It wasn't much, but it was enough. When Liz replaced the phone, she felt a reassurance in her own sanity that gave her the strength to face up to what was happening. Yet ironically Bridget Buscombe had also forced her to look into a darkness that chilled her to the core of her being.

What was in the house?

While Bill sketched away in his workroom, Liz thought quietly and rationally about their options. What was happening to them was beyond their comprehension. They had no knowledge of how to deal with a haunting and whatever was happening to Laurence, which was infinitely worse. The simple answer, then, was to find someone who did. She flicked through the telephone directory and located the number of the Catholic priest in Brecon. She felt a quiet desperation as she called, but in her heart she felt only faith could save them from whatever terrors lay ahead.

*

Bill's testimony: 'I was trying to look at every situation as being a coincidence, but there were so many of them – too many of them. I had the overwhelming sense of urgency that something was out of control, that we couldn't control. In other words, if we'd had a fire in the house, we could have put it out with an extinguisher or some water, but we couldn't deal with this nest of vipers or hornets, or whatever you choose to call it, by ourselves. There was this great fear going on that would not be there *all* the time, but it could happen most days, and for a while the feeling was so great it kept us all contained in the same bedroom. Even Laurence, because at the start, before he started to change, he was frightened too. There would be Liz and me, and baby Ben, and we made up a bed for Laurence at the foot of our bed. It was quite embarrassing for Laurence – he didn't really want to be with us and I quite understood that – but he said he was frightened and he consequently moved. There were humorous moments with the odd joke – it seemed to help. Nobody wanted to see or hear anything.

'How do you react? I think… we didn't react. This is something I used to do religiously every day: I would take Ben as a little baby down the road, in all weathers, in a pushchair for quite a long time in the day, thinking about what was happening in that house, trying to look at it in an intellectual way, trying to look at it in a common sense way, to make some sort of sense of the situation. After a while, I had to come to terms with the fact that I didn't understand it. At all.'

Chapter 4

The Catholic priest arrived on a turbulent night. A storm clattered across the hills and wind and rain lashed the trees around the house. He was a jovial man, slightly over-weight, quick to smile and softly spoken. Bill had picked him up from town because he couldn't drive, and on the way he chatted amiably as if nothing was amiss. In fact, on the phone he had accepted Liz's description of the haunting and its various manifestations with a serious, unsurprised manner, as if she was describing a leaking pipe. He had questioned her diligently about each sound and smell, paying particular attention to what factors Liz thought could have raised an unquiet spirit. When Liz had replaced the phone, she was left with the feeling that everything they had been through since November had not been unique, that, in fact, it was simply a regular part of the priest's job. On the one hand that bolstered her – they were not alone, not crazy – yet on the other, and in a much wider sense, it made her feel deeply uneasy.

Bill was in a very disturbed state when the priest shook off his dripping overcoat and stepped into the kitchen. The 'incidents', as he called them, had been worse in the period leading up to the priest's arrival. The footsteps had pounded manically through the house, the choking stench of sulphur materializing then disappearing. Most disturbing of all was the sense of that evil presence in every room, so powerful that Bill felt he could almost touch it. For the first time, he felt truly under threat; he feared for his life and his soul.

Laurence had locked himself in his room and refused to come out. The priest calmly told Bill and Liz he was going to bless each room and drive out whatever spirits were there. Spraying holy water around, he began in the kitchen, speaking in a low, yet powerful voice. The tension within Heol Fanog seemed to increase, as if there was going to be a thunderstorm within the walls. Bill and Liz led the way, holding each other's hands for comfort.

There were no bursts of sulphur, no sounds, no sense of conflict at all, but by the time the cleric had finished, the air of tension had drifted away like a mist dispersing in the sun.

The priest stayed for most of the night, reassuring Bill and Liz and praying. By the time he left they felt hope and optimism for the first time since November. And, indeed, the priest's blessing seemed to have worked, for they experienced no sounds or smells and felt no presence in Heol Fanog the next day, or for the following two days.

*

Liz's testimony: 'After the footsteps, it was the atmosphere of the house that changed. Rather than being a nice place to be, there was fear, and that fear affected every aspect of our lives, and our thoughts. When Laurence was at school in the day, Bill would be working in his studio and I'd take Ben in there and sit with him. One morning we heard this bloody noise that sounded awful. Like somebody laughing horribly. We ran out of the house and then we realized it was a goat, one of the noises they make in their throat. It was stupid and we laughed, but it showed what sort of state we were in. We were really terrified all the time. After the priest's visit our mood lightened, and we felt like we could go back to how we had been.'

*

On the morning of the fourth day, Bill drove into town while Liz took Ben for a walk in his pram, despite the chill in the air. It was early March 1990 and after the grey days of winter the brilliant blue sky seemed to match her optimism. She followed the lanes down to a little bridge over a stream and sat there for a while, hoping Bill's work would pick up now the house was free of the malign influence.

After an hour, she returned to Heol Fanog and was surprised to see from the empty drive that Bill was still not back from Brecon. They had arranged to eat lunch together at noon and Liz wondered if she should begin preparing the food.

As she pushed open the creaking gate and began to heave the pram over the ruts in the drive, Liz glanced up at the house and instantly felt a chill flood her system. There was a face framed in the tiny, dark window of the nursery. She saw it in such stark detail it was obvious it wasn't a trick of the light, and even though it faded after the initial contact of their eyes, Liz had no doubt that it had been there.

It was a woman, her face wrinkled with old age, yet a ghastly pale counterpointed by staring eyes like black pebbles. Her expression was one of great sadness. All of this Liz took in in an instant.

She pushed the pram as fast as she could to the door, and then snatched up Ben and listened for any sound. After a moment or two, and with her heart pounding madly, she started to climb the stairs.

*

Bill found Liz huddled in a corner of the landing, holding Ben tightly to her breast where he slept peacefully. Tears streaked her face and flared her cheeks scarlet.

'What is it?' he said, breathlessly, after bounding up the stairs.

She looked at him with pitiful, haunted eyes and said, 'It's not gone. It's still here.'

After Bill had led Liz down to the kitchen and made her a cup of tea, she told him what she had seen. Bill suggested it might have been her mind giving shape to random shadows and light on the panes, but Liz was adamant in her refusal; the old woman's face was burned into her memory, every wrinkle and crease, the pallor of her skin, the sadness in her eyes. And when Liz had investigated upstairs, every room was, of course, empty.

Bill allowed himself to relax, *feeling* the atmosphere in the house since he had arrived. Liz was right. The calm that had characterized Heol Fanog since the priest's blessing was gone. In its place was the familiar, edgy sensation rumbling in the background like distant, buried machinery; the air was oppressive, depressing, threatening.

The tension crept up his spine, strangling the happiness and relief he had enjoyed for the last three days. It hadn't gone away. It had only been in hiding.

After they discussed Liz's sighting further, Bill shook his head incredulously. 'Is that it, then? Everything we've been experiencing, all the strange things, what's happened to Laurence and the business, it's all been caused by the ghost of an old woman?'

'When I went in the nursery and it was empty, all I could feel was sadness,' Liz replied. 'Not evil. There wasn't that feeling that was always around before, that something was out to hurt us. From here face, and from how the room felt, it just seemed that she was really, really sad. All I thought was, You poor old thing. There was no malice intended. I had this impression she was thinking, What are you doing here? This is my place.'

'No malice?'

Liz shook her head.

'So what are you saying?'

She chose her words carefully. 'That she's part of it, certainly, but that she's not all of it.'

'There's more than one ghost?'

Liz nodded. Her face took on a weary fear that Bill had never seen before.

*

Bill and Liz spent the next few days researching the past occupants of Heol Fanog. The mother of the owner, Mr Holbourn, had lived in the house until her old age and deteriorating health had forced her to a residential home. But there had been other old ladies who had rented the place before Bridget Buscombe moved in during 1982. Their queries ignited a desperate desire to discover all they could about the house in the hope that it would unearth some explanation for their suffering; it was as if the rationalism of facts and figures and cause and effect could in some way counter the rampant fear they felt of being victim for *no* reason. That was the real terror: that supernatural forces could strike at any time and any place without a trigger.

They found a local historian in Brecon, and although she didn't know much about Heol Fanog's past she agreed to carry out some research on their behalf. At the same time, Bill wrote to the local newspaper, the *Brecon and Radnor Express,* and was interviewed about the haunting of Heol Fanog. He hoped that anyone who might know about the house's history would see the article and get in touch.

*

Soon after Liz saw the old woman, they started to experience problems in the toilet just off the hallway, the centre of so many of the strange happenings. It had happened overnight. That morning the toilet had wobbled in its setting and the floor around where the lavatory was seated upon the tiles began to lift up. Bill commented that there looked like there was something beneath the stones, trying to push its way up, and out. With everything else that had been happening in Heol Fanog, Bill couldn't help a shudder. But, as usual, he tried to think of every rational explanation: leaking pipes, rising water, water freezing and expanding upwards, even though there had been no frost.

The plumber came around at 11 a.m. and Bill left him alone to carry out his tests. He emerged from the toilet half an hour later, shaking his head. Strangely, the floor of the lavatory had subsided to its original position a quarter of an hour before he arrived. Like the men who had checked the septic tank when the sulphurous smells began, he could find nothing. The floor seemed solid and dry; there were no leaks beneath it. He re-seated the toilet and left.

Half an hour later, the toilet was loose once more and the floor was rising.

Bill phoned the plumber up, and as they talked the workman said something which immediately perked Bill alert. 'I've had enough of coming back to that place,' he sighed.

'You've been here before?'

'I worked there for a while in the sixties, putting in the central heating system. And there was something about the place…' he paused.

'Go on,' Bill said.

'I had a young apprentice working with me and he felt something. It was in late November or early December and the nights were drawing in early. We'd work until five and by that time it was already dark outside, and you know how lonely it is up there. Anyway, one night I told the lad I had to nip into Brecon early and he should finish up for the day on his own. He point-blank refused. He said he wasn't going to stay in that place on his own for anyone, even if I paid him more money. He said there was something funny about the place – he always felt someone was watching him. He was bloody scared, I could see it in his face.'

Bill's hand tightened on the phone; another sign that they were not alone in their experiences. That whatever was in Heol Fanog had been there for a long time.

'That's not all,' the plumber continued. His voice sounded suddenly strange, tense. 'I'm not a man who's easily spooked by things. I don't have much time for ghosties and ghoulies and things like that…' There was a long pause while he chose his words. 'The day after we'd put all the central heating system in, I got an angry call from the owner. I cam rushing up to the house and Mrs Holbourn showed me that all the radiators had come off the wall. All of them. Now I'm very particular about my work. I'm not slapdash. I knew we'd done a good job and there was no way that could have happened, but I set to fastening them all back on. I went round double-checking afterwards. And they were all solid. I told her, "I don't know what happened, but they're all safe as houses now." She thanked me and I set off, thinking that was the last of it.

‘The next day I got another call from her. It had happened again. By this time I knew there was something funny going on. Those radiators couldn’t have come off the wall unless someone had pulled them off, and I’m pretty sure the owner didn’t spend all night ripping them down just so she could bother me. So I went back up and fastened them all up again. Only this time I was remembering what the apprentice had said, and I admit I was starting to feel a bit funny.

‘And it just kept on doing it and doing it, night after night. I was getting more frightened by it, and the owner was starting to think I didn’t know what I was doing. I had to come up with something to stop it, see, and then I had this brainwave. I didn’t know what was causing it – I didn’t even want to think about that – but I suppose in my heart of hearts I must have known because I decided to fasten up all those radiators with cruciform screws. You know, screw with a cross cut in the end. And you know what?’ He paused. ‘It did the trick.’

The plumber sounded sincere, and there was no reason why he should be lying. Like Liz, when she had spoken to Bridget Buscombe, Bill felt comforted that the haunting had been taking place before they had arrived; it was reassuring to feel they had walked into the situation, instead of causing it in some way.

The plumber talked a little more and after a while he asked, ‘Do you know what might be causing it?’ There was a note of embarrassment in his voice; to ask the question was a recognition that what was happening couldn’t be explained rationally.

‘No,’ Bill replied. ‘No idea. Liz has seen an old woman about the place, but we don’t think she’s behind it all. I wish we did know. It would be easier to cope with if we had an explanation.’

‘You’ll find out,’ the plumber said reassuringly. ‘Everything will fall into place.’

Bill wasn’t so sure. He felt that what was in Heol Fanog was hiding from them, making its presence felt and then disappearing back into the shadows. It didn’t want to be found out.

*

The day the *Brecon and Radnor Express* came out with Bill's picture and interview, he was feeling low. The footsteps, the smells and the temperature changes had been ceaseless; it was like Chinese water torture, slowly driving him insane. He had reached a point where he felt what he and Liz now described as The Fear all the time, a constant tightening across the chest, sweats and shakes, a dread that something terrible was getting closer to him with each day, something hungry for his soul and his life. It was a madness that kept him on the verge of fleeing from the house and never returning; indeed, at that point he had finally decided Liz was right and he should give up his beloved studio and move the family somewhere else. They had reached their limit. They had to get out before something awful happened.

At mid-morning, a couple of hours after the paper would have gone on sale in town, Bill received a phone call from a local builder. At first the man was quiet and tentative, almost embarrassed. He said he was interested in what Bill had to say because he had had some experience of Heol Fanog himself. Bill's ears pricked up.

'I worked on the conversion of the house. I have to say I never felt any of the bad atmosphere you described in the paper. It just seemed like a normal house to me.'

Bill was instantly deflated. He had too much on his mind to waste time on someone who just wanted to say he was stupid. He started to make some apologies and prepared to put down the phone when the builder's tone changed.

'The old manor house next to it was a different matter altogether. It seemed very odd down there, it did. We used a lot of material from that place to convert the house. One thing that bothered me was we found lots of gravestones there. Big, old, black ones. They must have dated back years.'

Bill recalled what his neighbour had told him about the stones. It seemed the tale had been true.

‘I think there’s a cemetery there,’ the builder continued. ‘Probably just a little one, you know, for the manor house itself, like. It would be out at the back, in the garden…’

The builder seemed loath to say exactly what was on his mind – he was a down-to-earth man who wouldn’t countenance talk of the supernatural – but the meaning in his words was implicit. The cemetery had been disturbed. The stones had been used. What else had been disturbed?

*

While Bill worked in his studio, Liz would spend her days with Ben, doing everything she possibly could to stop herself thinking about what was happening around her. Yet it was hard; the house itself was a constant reminder. Things took a turn for the worst on a beautiful day, as winter turned slowly into spring at the twilight end of March. Although it was still chill, the sun was bright, dazzling between the tress and throwing wild patterns of light and shade across the area in front of the house.

Liz could see all that, yet she felt like she was looking at a TV showing some picture of a land a thousand miles away. The sunlight didn’t seem to penetrate the house at all; inside it was so gloomy the day felt like it was permanently on the edge of evening. That constant, oppressive shadow seemed to sap her energy and her hope. It was all she could bring herself to do to sit at the window and look out. Actually to venture out into the sunlight would take a monumental effort.

At that point Liz had a sudden thought of Ben asleep in his cot upstairs. Once he was old enough, they had moved him into his own room next to the stairs and he seemed to have settled into it well. She couldn’t hear him stirring, yet she had the strangest feeling that she had to see him.

It wouldn’t hurt to check in on him, just to put her mind at rest, so she rose and quietly climbed the stairs. Bill’s studio door was shut tight; no sound came from within. Liz crept along the landing, pausing outside the nursery to see if she could hear Ben within, and then she swung open the door.

Her attention wasn't drawn to the cot, but what was next to it. Sitting in the comfy chair where she would often feed Ben, was an old woman, a smudge of black and grey among the colour of the child's room. The woman Liz had seen at the window. Her wrinkled, pallid face was turned towards the sleeping figure of Ben as she watched him intently, her hands folded in her lap. Liz didn't really register her clothes except that they were black; the old woman vanished the moment Liz blinked.

She slumped against the door jamb in shock and horror, her heart pounding. The vision had been there for only the briefest instant, but it *was* unmistakably there. And even if Liz could force herself to disbelieve the evidence of her own eyes, the air was filled with a thick, dolorous sensation so powerful that Liz felt deflated and tearful. It was the old woman's trace, a psychic, emotional scent.

She *had* been there.

Liz scrambled out of the nursery and crashed into Bill's studio. He looked irritated that she had disturbed his sketching, but the moment he registered her terrified expression, he dropped his pencil and ran to her.

'What is it?' he hissed as he scooped her into his arms.

Liz could barely find her voice. 'I saw her,' she croaked. 'The old woman. She was sitting next to Ben's cot, looking at him. It was like she was so sad that we were around.'

Bill thought about what she said for a moment and then repeated almost in a daze, 'You saw her?'

First the footsteps, then the smells, then the temperature changes. Now apparitions.

Where would it end?

*

The dam they had erected to try to hold their lives steady could no longer continue under the strain; Liz's vision was all it took for the torrent to break through and engulf them. They dashed from the house that day and waited at the local council's housing offices until they were finally given an appointment. After filling in all the necessary forms, they huddled together in a booth and pleaded with a council official to be rehoused. Although the things that had been happening to them were as real as the council tax and electricity bills, they knew how it would sound to outsiders. Insane. After all, they could barely believe it themselves. For that reason, they were lost for an answer when the official repeatedly asked why they wanted to leave perfectly good rented accommodation for a council property.

In the end they started to babble about an 'uncomfortable presence' and 'being unhappy there,' but while the official agreed to process their application he made it plain there wasn't enough reason to provide them with a much in-demand council house. Outside the offices they desperately tried to think of an alternative way out. The failure of Bill's business meant they couldn't afford to buy a place. They could try and find another place to rent, but they knew how hard it had been to get Heol Fanog.

They had to face up to it: they were trapped.

*

The acceptance of their situation was the blow that reduced them to a black depression. How could they consider spending their days at Heol Fanog with so many awful things happening with increasing regularity, and the real fear that their lives were under attack? How could they cope? It was a question they bounced off each other repeatedly, but which had no answer. All they could agree was that they *had* to cope – for the children's sake.

Back at the house, Bill's mood was dashed even further. His final chance of work fell through. They had nothing coming in, and barely enough set aside to buy food for the next week or two. Although it left them even more isolated, they agreed they had to give up the phone; there was no way they could afford the bills.

That night they lay in bed like corpses, cold and still, staring into the dark but seeing no way out, dreading every second that something terrible would happen, listening to every creak as the wind roared around the house. Something was in there with them; they could both feel it.

And as the night drew on, Laurence lay in his red room next door, the TV turned up too loud, as yet another horror video played remorselessly, refusing all pleas to turn it down. The only response from him was a stream of bellowed abuse through the locked door. He was getting worse and worse; they never seemed to see him any more. They could just feel his presence like a black stain in the air.

And the noise made Ben cry, and however much Liz tried to calm him, he wouldn't shut up. And the night drew on.

The following morning Bill woke in agony. His hands felt like they had been put through a wringer. In the gloom of the bedroom it was impossible to see what was wrong so, still dazed, he staggered out on to the landing. For a moment he couldn't comprehend what he was seeing, and then slowly shock and disbelief broke through. The tips of his fingers were cracked and weeping; he could see blood there. There had been no sign of it the previous day.

Frantically, he searched for an explanation. An allergy to his paints, perhaps, although he had never exhibited one before. Anxiously, he hurried along to his studio to try and put his mind at rest, but his worst fears were confirmed. He couldn't manipulate a brush in any way without pain lancing up his fingers.

He stumbled back to the bedroom and woke Liz. She snapped from her half-awake state when she saw his hands thrust in front of her face. 'God, what is it?' she asked incredulously.

'I can't paint, Liz,' he replied in a cracked voice. 'It's stopped me painting.'

*

While Bill was at the doctor's surgery seeking treatment, Liz was at her wit's end. Making the most of the phone before it went, she called her mother, then various friends, desperately trying to seek some advice. Eventually, in desperation, her calls led her to an acquaintance who was a medium in Cardiff. The woman listened patiently to everything Liz said; it was the first time Liz felt she was not being judged when she tried to explain the madness they were experiencing.

In fact, the medium sounded almost as frightened as Liz when they discussed the details of the haunting, and in particular what was happening to Laurence. The medium refused to deal with the matter herself, but she insisted Liz call as a matter of urgency the head of the Christian Spiritualist Church in Cardiff. Liz asked her why she was so concerned, but she refused to go into any details. 'Just call Ray Williams,' she said.

Liz found the number and dialled. She was eventually put through to Ray Williams, who spoke very quietly and listened intently as she described what was happening in the house and the transformation that had come over Laurence.

'I will be up to visit at the earliest opportunity,' he said. 'I think it is important that we act quickly.'

When Liz asked him what he felt needed to be done for Laurence, he replied, 'I think he should be removed from the house immediately. For his own sake.'

*

Bill's testimony: 'Liz phoned up Ray Williams at the Christian Spiritualist Church in Cardiff and told him about Laurence's state of mind and he then told her that Laurence was responsible for the poltergeist phenomena. That's all it was as far as he was concerned – poltergeist phenomena. This Ray Williams, who's the head of the church, was not aware of exactly what was going on. He put everything down to Laurence's mother who had recently left him. He put it down to poltergeist phenomena that had come from a very angry teenager. I'd heard of that before and I quite accepted that. Every single thing that these people told us we believed, simply because we were moving in an area we didn't understand. We assumed that these people knew more than we did and that what they were saying was the truth. So on every step of the way it was becoming more and more intangible, and it was making less and less sense, and our poor little heads were spinning. In the end, to cope with it, we had to become more conscious of the reality – not the non-reality or supernatural reality – so we were concentrating on the changing of nappies and making cups of tea and doing little things like that. Turning our minds away from it all the time.

'Between April and June 1990, Laurence was getting so bad, I mean, unmanageable. He was spitting at me, he was swearing at me. He wasn't actually doing any violence or anything like that, but he was just being terrible unpleasant... and it was building up. It was *not* him – I can't stress that enough. I knew that afterwards. At the time, I just simply put that down to possibly him being... well, I don't know. I was trying to understand what was going on – something I couldn't understand.'

*

Bill slumped on the sofa in the lounge and stared blankly at the silent TV. The world was spinning out of control, and he had no idea what to do next. The doctor hadn't been able to explain what was wrong with his fingers, but he had given him an ointment to try to treat them. They were still weeping and they felt like a hammer had been slammed down on the end of each one. They had discussed the possibility of an allergy, but the doctor hadn't been convinced, and Bill knew in his heart that wasn't the answer. *It* had attacked one of the things closest to his heart, his one escape from the pressures of Heol Fanog, his painting.

And when he had returned to the house, he was horrified when Liz told him the spiritualists believed Laurence should be sent away. The blows had been delivered one-two style, only this one hit him deep in his heart. It was his *son*. How could he throw him out? But the madness that had afflicted Laurence was so great, he couldn't dismiss it out of hand, and that made the guilt cold and hard in his chest. Perhaps there was another way. Perhaps Liz had got it wrong. For so long his rational mind had searched for rational explanations. Laurence was just going through a phase. He would get over it. By the time Laurence's actions had got obviously out of hand, Bill didn't know who to turn to for advice. Was it his fault for not acting sooner? So many thoughts tumbled through his head, he couldn't think straight anymore, and he wished the spiritualists were there right then to put an end to his worries.

He looked up when Liz walked into the room. Her face was serious, but bright. She was holding something in her hand. He glanced at it, recognized it just as she spoke.

'Bill, I'm pregnant,' she said.

*

Ray Williams arrived one morning in April 1990, a slightly plump man of about fifty-five, with a whimsical manner. He was accompanied by Larry Harry and another man from the Christian Spiritualist Church in Cardiff. They sat in the living room and went through the events in Heol Fanog in detail with Williams focusing on Laurence's involvement.

When all the information had been laid out, Williams said he felt Laurence was the root cause. He described him as a 'confused individual' likely to have been responsible for sparking poltergeist phenomena in the house. For his sake, Williams reaffirmed that he felt it would be best if Laurence was taken away from the house, although he stressed that wouldn't end the phenomena; it would, however, help Laurence. The hangover of whatever Laurence had brought into Heol Fanog would have to be cleared in a different way.

Bill led the group up to his studio where he and Liz had their 'auras cleansed'. This involved the Riches sitting in the centre of the room while the spiritualists passed their hands around their bodies about six inches away from their skin. Afterwards the three men washed their hands and professed Bill and Liz 'clean'. They left soon after to make plans for return visits when they could 'treat' the house.

*

Liz's testimony: 'There was a very special way that I found Ray Williams. When I was in Cardiff, I lived and worked just down the road from a medium. Now at that stage, I was just trying to get out of anorexia and I thought this medium might be able to help. I'd tried everything else. So I went to see this woman. She used to do aura cleaning with her Red Indian spirit guide – it was bloody weird. But she was the only person I knew that dealt with such matters, so I phoned her up and explained what was happening. She said, "There's no way. I can't touch this." She said what you need to do is to get hold of Ray Williams and she gave me his phone number and I had a chat with him.

'In due course, Ray and Mr Harry came down. I wasn't here at many of these things because I removed myself with Ben – I didn't want him to see this sort of stuff going on at all. But I did talk to him on the phone about what he felt about Laurence, and I was there briefly while we had the auras cleansed. He felt it would be better if Laurence were removed from the situation because of the negativity. And he was, he was a negative influence. I know you hear a lot about when another woman marries the father, they want the kids out of the way. But it wasn't like that with me and Laurence. He was like my little brother – we get on incredibly well now. He'll tell me things that he won't tell his dad. But at that stage he was unbearable. He was a brat. He was certainly evil at one stage – I couldn't go near him. So I figured that Ray Williams was probably bloody well right. I think, in fact, that the Ray Williams thing was the best thing that could have happened to Laurence… for him to get the hell out of the situation.'

*

Bill and Liz needed a breathing space to build up their strength and the only bolt-hole available was Liz's mother's house. They fled early one morning, but although they left Heol Fanog behind, their thoughts returned to it constantly. After a couple of weeks, the spiritualists returned. They had discussed the Riches' case in depth and they felt more investigation was needed.

*

Bill's testimony: 'My own personal feeling was that after the spiritualists' first visit I certainly didn't feel any different as a result of the cleansing of the auras. Ray Williams didn't come again, but Mr Harry and the other man came a second time in the June. We weren't living in the house at that time because it was pretty horrible. We moved away for three weeks and I made this appointment for Mr Harry to come to the house over the telephone from my mother-in-law's house. I was to meet with them on a Saturday morning at eight o'clock. I was the first one there and I made a cup of coffee and waited.

'When they arrived, they were rather like me, incredibly nervous to the point that they were smoking incessantly. After a cup of coffee, the next thing they wanted to do was to walk around the property. They went right around the house itself, then outside the house. When we came to an area outside the back of the bathroom window, Mr Harry, in a rather dramatic way – I say dramatic rather than melodramatic, because he was a little bit like that, this particular character – he doubled up and almost fell over. He said he'd had a terrible shock in the middle of his back. Many other mediums and clairvoyants have found similar things at that particular site.

'Then we went back into the kitchen and they were ready to start doing whatever they were going to do. They went straight away into the middle of this most sensitive area in the house – between the loo and the bathroom in the hallway area. I was in the kitchen having another cup of coffee, but I could hear what was going on as they went into a trance. In this trance, they were laughing. I heard the word "Presbyterian". "You're not a Presbyterian. You're not a Presbyterian." That's very important because of what was about to follow.

'The whole period they were in a trance would be about twenty-five minutes and they came back into the kitchen and washed their hands. I said, "Can you tell me what the hell's going on? What have you found?" They said, "We've found four things here. There's an old lady who was trapped here, who couldn't get away from here. There was a mischievous young man and another young man.

They've all gone now. And then we found something that didn't want to go. It said that it was a Presbyterian, but we could see through it. Our spirit guides told us it wasn't a Presbyterian, but it was something quite opposite. It was something that had been conjured up from the sixteenth century because of what you had done in a previous life. We're not quite sure what you had done, but for sure we know you've upset an alchemist from that time. And this plague, this witch – we'll call it that for want of a better word that you'll understand – has been stuck on you."

'I asked for how long, and he said, "The information we have is for eighteen to twenty-two years." How do you feel when someone tells you something like that? Unfortunately I believed them. I really believed this was something. I believed them in the same way I believe a mechanic who tells me what's wrong with my car – they were supposed to know what they were doing. I went back to Cowbridge to see Liz and I gave her this information and I apologized to her for causing all this upset because it was my fault as a result of something I had done in a previous life. I believed it – and it took some believing. But that property did become better – for a week or so, anyway.'

*

The thought of a curse preyed on Bill's mind throughout his journey back to Cowbridge. On the one hand, the idea of an alchemist or a witch hexing him in a past life seemed too far-fetched, almost farcical. On the other, it provided an explanation for his gut feeling of victimization and it fitted in with a deep-seated yet inexplicable guilt that he was in some way responsible for events in Heol Fanog. And was a curse any stranger than the things they had experienced in that lonely house? Liz, however, told him to forget such thoughts instantly. She was adamant that the spiritualists were wrong. 'It's ridiculous, Bill. You're not to blame,' she told him. 'This kind of thinking will only make matters worse. There's another explanation, and once we find that, everything will be clear.'

*

The testimony of Ray Williams of the Christian Spiritualist Church, Cardiff: 'I lost touch with Mr Harry after the events at Heol Fanog. It was just a one-off thing for me, but Larry was very much more involved. I don't remember what was wrong exactly, but I know there was some disturbance at the house. Over the years, many people called us because they were experiencing some kind of problem of this type. We would visit to establish what was wrong and if there was a spirit there, try to help that spirit. And when that had been done, the disturbance should cease.'

*

It was a wrench for Bill and Liz to return to Heol Fanog, but they had no other option. When they arrived back from Liz's mother's, its oppressive atmosphere was as potent as ever. In July 1990 the Riches received three strange guests. It was a hot, sunny Saturday and, as usual, Bill and Liz were desperate to get out of Heol Fanog, so they had planned to drive into Cowbridge with Ben for lunch with Liz's mother. Laurence remained at the house, but at that stage Bill and Liz were barely communicating with him. He was isolated in the anger that seemed to be with him at all times. Later, however, he told them what happened.

Just after leaving, Bill encountered a large Renault coming in the opposite direction. The lanes aren't wide enough to pass so he had to reverse a long way to let the car by, cursing what he thought were tourists. The Renault continued to the house and pulled up outside. The driver, a man in his fifties with rings covering his fingers, and his two companions, both attractive women in their twenties, were foreign, but not tourists.

*

Laurence's testimony: 'They came up to the house and I met them at the door. They were weird-looking. The two women were tartily dressed and the man was tall and oldish and tanned. They were French. They said they were registered exorcists who were living in the Pyrenees. The man wanted to meet Bill and Liz, but I said they'd just missed them and they looked disappointed. The man claimed he'd dreamed of the house and what was happening in it and the dream told him to get to Heol Fanog as soon as possible. They'd set off immediately and had got the ferry over, but he said he couldn't stay because he had to get the ferry back that evening. The man and the women talked to each other for a bit and then they asked if they could have a look round the house. They went from room to room and then around the garden, talking to themselves. They said something about a black cat and a stone cross and that the answer lies underground – a pagan burial ground. After a while, they went back to the hall where the man got out a compass. I looked at it with him and it went wild. It was just spinning and spinning. After that, they thanked me and left.'

*

Such surreal interludes became the norm for Heol Fanog over the following months. The house seemed to attract a range of colourful, eccentric individuals who had their own peculiar theories as to what was behind the house's menacing phenomena. There was one thing which united all of the disparate characters, however – their belief that Heol Fanog's power was dark, and growing.

Chapter 5

The injury to Bill's fingers was debilitating, yet it set off resonances that disturbed the Riches on a much more fundamental level. It seemed too closely linked to everything else the family had experienced. What better way to attack Bill than to strike at the source of his income and the heart of his being. Bill lived to paint – it was an obsession which only artists could understand – and suddenly he could no longer do it. Sometimes, when he felt the urge to rush to his studio and create something, he would look at his weeping, raw fingers and feel the pressure build inside him until it seemed like it was going to tear him apart. There was no release, and so the energies stayed inside, turning black, poisoning him.

The Riches desperately tried to force it to be a simple coincidence. An allergic reaction to his paints, to washing-up liquid. Some bizarre virus. Bill went to his doctor repeatedly, and then for numerous tests at the hospital. A homeopath prescribed an ointment. Nothing worked; no explanation could be found. His fingers grew so painful, he wondered briefly if it would cripple him forever. As the days went by, Bill's depression increased, turning towards despair. He spent his time trying to take some of the burden off Liz – cleaning, cooking, shopping.

And then, one morning, he woke up and the mysterious ailment had disappeared. He felt as if he had been taken to the brink and shown the abyss and then brought back with the knowledge of what was there and what he had to lose. A torment directed at the very heart of him.

Although he didn't know it then, it was not the end of it. The illness returned many times over the years, always when he least expected it. And it took much more than a doctor's prescription to rid him of it for good.

*

In the cauldron of their troubles, the only place Bill felt safe was in his studio. His painting was a talisman that kept the dark at bay;

when he was working he could drive all other thoughts out of his head. He had finished the gridplan sketch of his masterwork and he was ready for that incandescent moment when he would begin to apply the oils to the blank canvas. He was pleased with the results of his planning; the intricacy of the design made the work a complex piece which he knew would speak on many levels. He hadn't shown it to Liz yet – he wanted to surprise her with what he was certain would be his best work to date.

With the thump of the blood in his brain, he began to paint the first image – a still-beating heart.

*

In July 1990, the phone was finally cut off. They were truly isolated.

Liz went to her mother's with Ben for a break from the stress and strain; in that atmosphere her pregnancy was wearing her out and she needed a rest. Bill remained in Heol Fanog with Laurence, although their spheres rarely intersected. Bill could barely bring himself to stay in the house, where the quiet was regularly punctuated by footsteps or slamming doors, yet he didn't want to leave Laurence on his own. He still made repeated attempts to build bridges between them as he battled with his own guilt that he was throwing his son out, but Laurence never responded.

It was a warm, damp morning, with the sun breaking through streaked clouds, when Bill glanced out of the kitchen window and saw Mr Harry and a middle-aged couple walking slowly up the drive. Relieved to have company of any kind, Bill met them at the door.

The spiritualists had been discussing Heol Fanog during a seminar at the church in Northcote Street, Cardiff, when the man and woman, who were Dutch, had felt an inexplicable urge to visit, Mr Harry explained. He had tried to phone, but on discovering the line cut off, they had driven to Brecon without an appointment because of the Dutch couple's sense of urgency. Bill welcomed them in eagerly.

As the couple wandered around the house and gardens, Mr Harry sat with Bill in the kitchen and told him they wanted to try something which those in the seminar felt would cure the problem. Mr Harry called it 'creating a psychic wall'.

'Do anything,' Bill told him. 'Anything at all. I don't care what it is. If there's a chance it will work, that's good enough for me.'

As they finished talking, the woman walked in and stated that she had 'seen something'. The visitors were both mediums, Mr Harry said; their sensitivity to the spirit's world was acute.

The woman claimed she had uncovered the spirit of a witch, tall, blurred and very fuzzy, but a potent presence. When Bill asked how she knew it was a witch, she said it was because the figure had been wearing a black, conical hat like the witches of mythology. The woman also claimed she felt the number seven was important. She got very excited when she probed Bill to find out if the number had any personal significance. The only thing he could thing of was his pet pig, which had been put down a few weeks earlier, had seven rings in its nose.

At that point, the man entered the kitchen with a curious expression. He had been wandering around the house on his own, but had lingered for an inordinate amount of time in the barn. He asked Bill if he knew anything about a history of witchcraft at Heol Fanog. Bill replied that he didn't.

'I saw part of a coven here. In the barn,' the man continued. 'Seven witches.'

*

The spiritualists wandered the sunlit garden for what seemed like an interminable period. When they returned to Bill at the doorway in the back of the barn, they were grim-faced and anxious. He asked them what was wrong and they told him they felt tremendous power – dark power – in the land itself. They were convinced the house had been erected on a sacred site dating back to pre-Christian times. Possibly, they thought, a pagan burial ground.

Remembering what the French exorcists had told Laurence, Bill was interested in what they had to say, but he found it hard to believe wholeheartedly, without any evidence other than a 'feeling'. He knew the history of the area. Celtic tribes had roamed across the Beacons above the Usk valley, which was too thickly wooded for any settlement, so it was *possible* that it could be a pagan site. However, he felt he needed a more tangible explanation.

The spiritualists weren't deterred by his obvious lack of enthusiasm for their insight, and continued to muse. Heol Fanog was on a powerful spot, they said, because it is a confluence of three ley lines. The earth's magical power was at its most potent there, which, they felt, could explain why the Celts had used it as a burial ground. In their view, ghosts are attracted to such a spot, as well as other entities that exist in the realms beyond day-to-day reality.

Bill was intrigued by their views, but it still didn't grab him. Yet as they sat in the dark kitchen, where the threatening mood was at its most powerful, the spiritualists' insights took on more credence. They certainly believed what they were saying – Bill could see it in their faces. Could he afford to discount it? Slowly their words began to eat their way into him.

They returned once again to the curse on Bill and reaffirmed they felt *he* was at the heart of the problem the family were experiencing. The curse was passed down through the Rich blood, they stressed, and had afflicted him first, about twenty years ago.

At other times, when he felt stronger, Bill might have dismissed the concept, but at the moment it appealed to his feelings of injustice. Bill replied that, yes, things had started to go badly for him about twenty years ago, and his father had suffered incredibly bad luck for at least fifty years, which seemed to be getting worse. Bill thought of the collapse of his business, how orders were suddenly withdrawn for no reason, how everything fell apart with such speed that market forces couldn't explain it.

The spiritualists asked Bill for information about his family history in case there was any clue to the origin of the curse. 'My family is of Romany extraction,' he began. 'There have been many remarkable people among my relatives, but the most remarkable, I suppose, was my great-great-grandmother who died at eighty-nine, having had four husbands and twenty-two children, and having been the first woman to sail around Cape Horn. My mother had two brothers, both of whom died in World War II, while my grandmother on my father's side was a doctor who was struck off in the thirties and forties for doing abortions. My father had a long service in the RAF and he was one of the first to be decorated in World War II. He is,' he added, 'very sceptical about all this.'

'Tell us about yourself, Bill,' Mr Harry said. 'Is there something in *your* past?'

Bill thought hard and then said tentatively, 'When I was a student I lived in a flat where the caretaker was Alex Saunders, who used to be known as the King of the Witches back then. He was quite infamous. He offered to make me a witch so I could be successful as a painter. The thought appealed to me at first and I started the initiation, but I pulled out part of the way through. I realized that, although I'd always been searching, it wasn't what I wanted.' He paused and thought about he said. 'Do you think that's it? That I'm paying for thinking about being a witch?'

The spiritualists couldn't answer for sure. Even so, the idea of a curse triggered something in his head and the wheels were set in motion.

*

Mr Harry and the Dutch man spent almost half an hour walking around the perimeter of the property. Bill watched them from the window, their heads bowed in deep thought or trance, muttering quietly. When they had finished their circumnavigation, Mr Harry told Bill the psychic wall had been erected; the house was now protected.

But the spiritualists' work was not completed. Bill, already destabilized by the events in Heol Fanog, had been thrown completely off-balance by the arrival of Mr Harry and his colleagues, battered by the information they kept throwing his way.

He felt almost dazed and the only response he could find within him was to accept blindly everything he was told and asked to do. Before they could leave, the spiritualists said, they had to carry out a ritual of cleansing.

The Dutch man marked out a pentacle on the kitchen floor, drawn in one movement, which he said was necessary for their protection. While he did this, his wife stood in the kitchen with outstretched arms to form the shape of the cross 'to prevent anything entering'. Incense was lit in the points of the pentacle, and then the man called on the spirits not to attack, to leave the house immediately. The ritual continued for several minutes, during which time Bill felt he was slipping further into some wild dream.

When it was over and they all felt psychologically and spiritually drained, Mr Harry and the Dutch couple shook Bill's hand and said they hoped Heol Fanog was now cleansed. They insisted that any time Bill or Liz were afraid, they should draw a pentacle on the stone floor, light joss sticks around it, and climb in for protection. Then they drove away, leaving Bill feeling like a whirlwind had passed through his life.

*

Later, he discussed the spiritualists' visit with Liz.

'Not the curse again?' she laughed. 'Don't be so silly. I thought we'd put that idea to rest. You're just trying to blame yourself for what's happened. And it's not you – it's the house.'

'Is it?' he said doubtfully. Liz could see the spiritualists' words had disturbed him deeply, but he wouldn't discuss the matter any further. He left her and continued to brood alone in his studio.

*

Bill's testimony: 'It was like a problem with your car. You can take it to a garage. Who else is going to sort it out – I can't do it? We were doing the same with the house. We were taking it to various different people on various different dates. We were treating the whole thing like that. We weren't going to sleep on the situation, but we were actually asleep in a sense, psychologically. We didn't want anything to hurt us, so we were conscious of simply bringing in people who we thought could help with our problem. It was so hard in the beginning to try to find them, but once they get to know about you, they all come…

'I was still very cautious about these spiritualists and I certainly didn't accept everything they said at face value. When the Dutch man said he had seen seven witches and then his wife went somewhere else and said she had seen one witch, I had the presence of mind to take the woman into the living room on her own to ask her what the witch looked like. She replied, "Tall and black with a conical hat – exactly like you'd expect." This was without the husband knowing what I was doing with his wife. Then I went to him and said the same and he replied, "Tall, black with pointed hats." He said they were very, very blurred and fuzzy, but there were seven of them. So at face value, they had both seen the same thing.'

*

Despite his ambivalence about what had happened that morning, there was certainly a change within Heol Fanog. In the space of a couple of hours, the whole place seemed to have grown bigger, brighter. The sunlight, which filled the garden, streamed in through the windows, and the black mood that thundered through the oldest part of the house faded completely. Over the following days, Bill and Liz were amazed by the transformation that had happened on so many levels. Suddenly there was no sense of anyone watching them, no feeling of evil. There were no footsteps, no smells, no temperature changes. And then Bill received his first commission in weeks, from some neighbours, the Gandys, who owned horses. They wanted Bill to paint a portrait of their favourite horse. Bill couldn't believe his luck. Once more the future looked bright.

*

Their happiness was marred by one morning of sadness and guilt as they packed Laurence off from the house. Bill's ex-wife, Denise, regularly visited Heol Fanog to see Laurence. Her relationship with

Bill and Liz was tense, but they remained cordial for Laurence's sake. Denise refuted Bill's view that their son was possessed; she felt he was simply acting like a normal, troubled teenager. He was still doing reasonably well at school and his teachers were happy; it seemed his problem behaviour was confined to the immediate vicinity of Heol Fanog. However, Denise agreed he should be removed from the house for his own good. She found a good boarding house in Brecon, where they knew he would be well-treated. It was only ten minutes away by car so they could see him easily.

Bill's emotions were in turmoil. 'Liz, I'm sending away my son,' he said pitifully, as they waited in the kitchen for Laurence to complete his packing. 'It can't be right. Lord, what am I doing?'

When he closed his eyes he could see Laurence's face at the moment he told him he would have to move out. In that instant, there was no evil there, no blind rage. It was just his fifteen-year-old son, to whom he had brought bacon and eggs in bed and gone for long walks in the country. His son, whom he loved and who loved him, now looking shattered and abandoned. There had been tears in his eyes, the first Bill had seen for months, and although Laurence never said a word, which was almost worse than what had gone before, Bill could see his thoughts in his face: 'You don't want me. You never wanted me. When you found Liz I became surplus to requirements. Now you're throwing me out so you can give all your time to her.'

Bill tried to explain that it was in Laurence's best interests, but the words sounded hollow in the face of such powerful emotions. He could barely believe it himself.

It had stayed with him for days and he was still beating himself with it there in the kitchen. It would have taken only the slightest excuse for him to call it all off and keep Laurence with them.

Liz grabbed his hand as she saw the conflict in his expression. 'Remember, Bill,' she said softly.

And he did. The spitting. The swearing. But most of all the change in Laurence's features where the thing had crawled into him and taken root.

'But what if it's all over now? Things have changed.'

'Can we take that chance? For Laurence's sake? Can we let him go any farther down that road he was travelling until we lost him completely?'

Lose him completely. Bill shook his head. 'We're fighting for his soul, aren't we?'

Liz nodded. 'Look, Bill, he's close by. We can see what happens to him. If there's no change in him we can bring him back and try to find another solution. But if there is a change – '

'We know it's the house.' He paused. 'The damned house.'

Still, when Bill climbed into the car and set off down the lane with a silent Laurence at his side, his heart broke in two.

*

Bill's testimony: 'That was a terrible time. I had to say to Laurence that it had been suggested by these people that he was not the cause of the problem, but he was making it a little bit worse and it might be necessary for him to move out of the house. And for me to have to do something like that to my own son just destroyed me. I only did it because Mr Ray Williams said so. I knew that in some way Laurence must have thought that I was thinking more of Liz than him, and that was something I had never wanted him to think. It certainly wasn't true – he was my number one. I was at my wit's end, but his mother, my ex-wife, managed to find a very nice boarding house in Brecon town for him to stay in and paid for by the Social Security fund because by that time our money had run out. He was there for about six months, and then he left school and managed to get a job as a washer-up at a local hotel.'

*

Bill coped with his emotional upset in the only way he knew how, by immersing himself in his painting. When things were going well, he lost himself in his creative energies so deeply he was almost in a trance. The images came from deep within his subconscious directly into his hands. He barely recognised what he was painting until he finished and stepped back to examine his work, and sometimes the shock was almost staggering.

The Gandys had provided him with a photograph of their favourite horse to work from, and Bill was eager to get the commission underway. After he had provided rough work on the horse's outline, he decided to go out to search for a good background. He wandered along the lanes around the Gandys' property and eventually found a field with a breath-taking backdrop of the Beacons.

As he settled down to sketch and photograph, a local farmer walking his collie stopped to glance over Bill's shoulder. Bill knew him vaguely – certainly as well as you could know any neighbour in a place where great distance made it impossible to lean over the fence and chat – and gradually they began talking. While the farmer was mildly curious about Bill's work, Bill was more than interested in what the farmer had to tell him about the problems the locals had suddenly started experiencing.

A blight had descended on the area. Lambs and calves were being born blind, deformed or deaf; the farmers had never experienced anything like it before. Vets were baffled, and everyone was afraid their business would be decimated.

Bill listened intently and then asked exactly when the problem seemed to have started. The farmer counted back the days on his fingers to the first deformed birth. It was the day after the spiritualists claimed to have erected the protective psychic wall around Heol Fanog.

Coincidence, Bill told himself as he made his way back to the house. But that was all there had been since that first night they had heard the footsteps. Coincidence heaped upon coincidence upon coincidence until the word lost all meaning. In isolation, everything could be taken with a pinch of salt; together they formed a mountain that the mind found it difficult to climb.

*

The painting came on in leaps and bounds. Bill found himself enthused, almost driven, for the first time since the troubles had started. It was the house – it seemed just like it was the first day they moved in. Liz remarked on it too, mentioning the magical dome which seemed once again to keep them all secure and happy. Gradually, they found themselves believing that everything was going to work out, their dream resurrected, yet Bill felt a strange, nagging doubt like a twist in his stomach that prevented him from committing himself completely. He couldn't shake what the farmer had told him; there was no reason for it to bother him, but the description of the blight had its hooks in his psyche.

He cursed angrily and forced himself to focus on the painting. He was having trouble with one of the horse's rear legs, never an easy task at the best of times with its oppositional joints. Yet however many times he painted over it to correct whatever it was that looked wrong, it always came out the same. It was as if his hand was preventing him from putting it right. His difficulty with the leg continued for several days, with Bill becoming increasingly infuriated. In the end, he had to admit defeat. He had got the leg as close to what it should look like as possible, and, with the magnificent, powerful background, it was barely noticeable.

When he delivered it to the Gandys, they were overjoyed. Bill had excelled himself, they said. They also remarked on how well Bill was looking. They had been aware of what was happening in Heol Fanog almost from the onset when Bill had started to quiz them about previous strange occurrences in the house. Over the months, they had witnessed his deterioration from the confident, positive man who had moved in, to someone who seemed not only nervous, worried and depressed, but almost crushed by events. The speed of that transformation had disturbed them, and they regularly about what was taking place within the home of their nearest neighbour.

Bill told them it was all over now. He didn't go into detail about the spiritualists' psychic wall – he still couldn't quite believe it himself – but he simply said they had some help to rid the house of its threatening presence. The Gandys seemed relieved too, and with their peace of mind established they turned their attention back to deciding on the location to best show off their new painting.

Sick of their isolation, Bill and Liz scrimped and saved to get their phone reconnected. Their first call was from Mrs Gandy. She told Bill that their favourite horse, the subject of his painting, had died suddenly. Bill commiserated, but as they talked he thought he noticed a faint accusatory tone in her voice. When he queried her about it, she paused for several beats, as if deciding whether to answer, and then when she did the blame was unmistakable in her words.

The horse had injured one of its legs, the one Bill had had problems with in the painting. Despite the ministrations of the vet, and against all expectations, the horse's condition had worsened. In the end, the leg had looked misshapen, twisted, just how Bill had painted it. When it died from complications brought about by the injury, because of its size, the Gandys had buried where it fell. It was only afterwards, when they stood tearfully over the grave, that they realized it had died in exactly the same spot Bill had painted in the picture. Exactly, to the position of the hills, the trees and the hedgerows. The location he had chosen at random for its beautiful backdrop.

'And,' Mrs Gandy said in a cracked voice before putting down the receiver, 'everything you described happening in Heol Fanog has happened to us.'

Bill felt cold as he listened to the buzzing of the empty line, and then the chill turned to guilt. They had driven it out of Heol Fanog, but it had simply gone elsewhere – into the surrounding locale. The blighted animals. The dead horse.

It was as if it was displaying spite at being excluded from the house, showing its power was still potent and others would suffer for Bill's actions. As if it was saying it would never leave.

Never.

Later, the Gandys told Bill they had burnt his painting. They never called him again.

*

Basil Gandy's testimony: 'It was a very strange thing and I must admit we were a bit worried about what happened. You could call it coincidence, I suppose, but I try to keep an open mind about these things. We gave Bill a photograph of Echo, who was a valuable and much treasure black cob – and admittedly it wasn't a very good photo. In Bill's painting there was an illusion in the way the leg had been painted that made it looked like it had swelled up. A few days later, Echo developed a problem in the same leg. We got a vet it, but he treated the ailment with steroids, but that only made the problem worse. When we got another vet to give a second opinion he saw what was really wrong, but by then it was too late to save her. The leg looked exactly as it did in the painting.

'We don't blame Bill for what happened. We were aware of what was going on in Heol Fanog because Bill and his wife told us about it. And there *was* something happening there – you could see it in their faces.

'I filled Bill in about some gravestones from Heol Fanog which he found. When we came here about six years ago, we had some work done which involved taking out a very large wall and also involved lifting some concrete. Underneath we found a lot of broken gravestones. Local farmers used to pinch them, break them up and use them for ballast. We put them back together as best we could and they dated back to around 1750. They were all beautifully carved and in very good condition, so we put them out in the barn away from the elements. They told a very interesting story. They had all been brought up from Heol Fanog where there was a chapel and a graveyard next to the manor farm. Many of these old manors had their own private chapel. The gravestones seemed to cover the whole history of the Watkin-Jones family who lived there. There were a lot of early deaths – 4-year olds, 12-year olds, 46-year olds –

but I suppose in the 1700s they didn't have access to very good medicine. Still, it was an interesting find.'

*

Bill's testimony: 'We didn't have any problems for a while – everything was fine. But it wasn't with our neighbours – everything was going wrong. All that time they had blight on their sheep. They were born deformed, blind or dead.

'I was very pleased about the commission from the Gandys, even though I wasn't getting much for it. I got one of the horse's legs wrong at the back. I hate doing horse's legs – they are pretty weird things to have to paint. The horse died of some infection that they can pick up through their hooves, but this particular creature had picked it up on one hoof which made the back leg swell up. That was shown in the painting when the horse was in its prime. Where the horse fell down dead was where they buried it – horse are very heavy things – and the view from the place where the horse died is the same one as in the painting, and they burned the painting as a result. Sue Gandy said it looks to me that everything you've been talking about that's happening in your house is happening with us – everything is going wrong. It's a very sensitive issue, this particular horse of hers. They blamed me for it because I had put a hex on that horse.

'Again, I was thinking, What the fucking hell is going on here? These people have put a psychic wall around the property and now all hell is breaking loose with our neighbours. And the spiritualists were aware of it and one felt so guilty. It was really our fault. That was another pressure. But that was the parting of the friendly neighbour bit. They virtually cut off the relationship with us and that's why we're not really terribly close to them any more. It's of their doing, certainly not ours.'

*

Across from the front of Heol Fanog's property, a stream runs. During the summer it is often dry, as it had been for a short while that summer since the spiritualists claimed to have established their psychic wall. One day in August 1990, after the Riches had had several weeks of peace, storms broke over the hills and the rain came down in sheets, sloughing off the Beacons and bringing the dry stream to life. It gushed across the property one afternoon, and to Bill it was as if the water crossing the land destroyed the psychic wall.

The thing came back.

*

Although they never experienced the footsteps, temperature changes and smells again, the other manifestations, which had almost destroyed their lives over the previous spring, returned in force: the sense of a malignant presence watching them, the occasional glimpses of an old woman passing through the house. Bill and Liz felt crushed. It was like being told you were cured of a terrible illness, only to find a few days later that it was back. And this time, in some way, it seemed to be worse.

Liz was five months pregnant and it instantly placed her under tremendous pressure. They both felt they had to respond instantly. They agreed they had had enough of the spiritualists; they never felt entirely comfortable with them, either as people or with the work they did. Instead they decided to turn to an Anglican vicar, and the local church eventually directed them to one who could help.

The Reverend Bryn Jones was the vicar of Trallong, just outside Brecon. He was a quiet, thoughtful man in his late fifties, with receding silver hair. Bill and Liz went round to the vicarage and told him everything; it came out in a gush of anguish and terror, an unburdening of all the pressures that were crushing them down. Mr Jones listened without making any comment, and when they had finished, he simply said he would get back to them.

Bill and Liz felt desperate; they didn't know how much longer they could cope, but that evening at 6.30 p.m. there was a knock at the door. On the step were Mr Jones and two other men. One of them, a very tall man, at least 6ft 8ins, hung back, but the other introduced himself as the Reverend Roy Matthews of the Holy Trinity Church in Abergavenny.

As they walked into the living room, Bill noticed Mr Matthews was suddenly looking disturbed and glancing furtively around the room. Bill began to repeat what he had told Mr Jones that morning. Mr Matthews grew more and more uncomfortable with each passing moment. After ten minutes, he suddenly dashed from the living room, through the kitchen to the foot of the stairs.

Bill and Liz heard his anxious voice echo back.

'Stop! You can't hide from me! I can see you!'

As they followed him, he darted up the stairs and they heard him crash into Bill's studio. 'I can see you!' he shouted. 'You're hiding behind the easel.'

Bill and Liz looked at each other and stifled a snigger; his manner seemed bizarre, almost a joke. When he came back down, he said simply. 'They thought I couldn't see them, but I could.' Feeling bewildered, Bill and Liz were led into the living room and Mr Matthews beckoned to them to kneel for a prayer session. After several minutes, he began to talk in a low, calm voice.

'I am going to close these doors that have been opened,' he began. 'And I want you all to go through.'

Bill felt a shiver run through him; the air seemed uncommonly cold.

'One,' Mr Matthews continued, counting off the spirits he had seen. 'Two. Three.' There was a long pause and then he added, 'What about you? You're not escaping.'

After the ritual he explained to Bill that he had found three human spirits in the house, but the fourth was 'inhuman' – a demonic entity. It took more than fifteen minutes for Mr Matthews to remove this from the house, he said. Certainly, he had been holding a one-sided conversation for that length of time, growing increasingly agitated as if he was fighting some terrible mental battle, while Bill and Liz looked on from their praying position. By the end, Mr Matthews appeared drained, but he was confident he had driven the entity from Heol Fanog. He ended by calling on the blood of Jesus to protect the house and 'to bind Satan'.

*

Bill's testimony: 'Roy Matthews claimed to have found three human entities in the house – two young men and an old woman. Then there was what I will call the demonic thing. Anyway, he claimed to have done the job. Just as they were leaving and I was standing on the bottom step of the stairs, he stopped suddenly and said, "Oh, just let me do this." And he touched my forehead with his thumb. I said, "What are you doing?" And he said there was a fiery dart in my forehead. At the time I didn't know what he was talking about, but you can read about this in Ephesians in the Bible. "The shield to quench the fiery darts of the wicked one." I had one of these psychic arrows or fiery darts that the wicked one can launch. You know… you believe what these people are telling you…'

*

As happened after the Catholic blessing and the spiritualists' psychic wall, Heol Fanog enjoyed a period of grace following Mr Matthews' visit. Once again it was light, airy and peaceful, and all the phenomena ceased overnight. It was not even just a physical change; the atmosphere in Heol Fanog was normally so malignant that when it wasn't there Bill and Liz felt as if a blanket had been whipped from their heads. Their previous experience, however, had convinced them not to be too optimistic, and that proved to be the right attitude. In November 1990, three months later, everything returned in force.

Bill phoned Roy Matthews and he came round immediately, but on his own time this time. He spent an evening, going from room to room, and at the end, and looking exhausted, he said to Bill, 'It was hiding from me, but I have bound it.'

There was another respite, but this time for just a matter of days, and when Bill called Mr Matthews to see if there was anything else he could do, he admitted there wasn't. They would have to look elsewhere.

*

Things, however, *were* getting worse. Bill and Liz were witnessing more and more manifestations. One morning, while Liz was in the kitchen preparing some food for Ben, she glanced out the window and saw someone standing in the trees in front of the house. The figure was watching the house intently.

Liz ran out, yelling, but by the time she had reached the spot whoever had been there had vanished. She searched the area, but there was no sign of anyone and no flattened grass where the figure had been standing. She might have been able to dismiss it as a prowler if not for the fact that she saw it in the same spot again. And again. And again. Each time it became increasingly obvious that it was not physical.

The birth of Liz's second child, Rebecca, on 19 December 1990 went relatively smoothly compared to Ben's delivery. Yet when she returned home from the hospital, Liz was suddenly made aware of how the house affected everyone who entered it. Her mother, Eileen Sanders, had stayed in Heol Fanog with Bill and his mother to help with the care of Ben.

*

Liz's testimony: 'I stayed in the hospital just one night after Becca's birth, and then I came home. The atmosphere, when I opened this bloody door, could be cut with a knife. My mother was causing friction with Bill's mother, Bill was causing friction with my mother, and it was like the house was winding everything up. I thought, Bloody hell, I've just had a baby. Can't it just be nice for once? Just once. And it was exactly the same when my third, Tomas, was born.

'There was all this friction going on here. Later, my mother told me that she wanted to kill Bill. She said words were being put into her head to kill him. She only realized afterwards. She couldn't understand the hate. She doesn't get on with Bill and he doesn't get on with her, but it's never been at that level. But as they were going down the lane away from the house, she said it cleared, and she said she couldn't understand how she could have possibly felt like that to somebody else.'

*

While many of the initial problems disappeared with the spiritualists' visits, they seemed to have been replaced by the visual manifestations – apparitions that were infinitely more terrifying than what had gone before. It was rarely that Bill or Liz saw them full on. Sometimes they were only glimpses out of the corner of the eye or shapes seen at a distance among the thick foliage around the house. Shapes. Figures. They would come from nowhere and disappear just as quickly.

The old woman was the only one who appeared inside the house. Liz saw her on five occasions. The spiritualists also saw her, once, and their description matched Liz's exactly. One day while Bill was rearranging furniture in the studio, he came across a photo at the back among the furniture left by Heol Fanog's owner Mr Holbourn. There was a moment of *frisson* and then he rushed out to find Liz. The instant she saw the picture she exclaimed, 'That's her!'

The resemblance made her shiver – the face, the hair, the clothes. It was exactly how Liz had witnessed her standing next to the cot. It was Marion Holbourn, the owner's mother.

*

Though the apparitions were disturbing, most of them were too far away or glimpsed too quickly to be really terrifying, and the old woman in the house was more a vision of sadness. Yet the Riches couldn't shake the feeling that things were getting worse. The apparitions were another turn of the screw after the footsteps and the smells, and Liz had the vague, frightening feeling that the ones outside the house were drawing closer. She wondered how long it would be before something else appeared in the house itself.

*

Liz's testimony: 'It was shortly after Christmas 1990. Becca was in a carrycot and Ben was in the push-chair. I was bringing them in from outside. As I stepped into the hallway, I had a real shock. I saw this black silhouette of a seven-foot man walking just on the inside of the kitchen door, just passing the doorway. By that time, the way I responded had changed. The fear didn't dominate and I'd become totally numb to what had been going on – everything that was happening was starting to become relatively normal in a way. I went into the kitchen and it wasn't there. I knew it wouldn't be there – that's why I went in. The figure had been there, certainly – but these things happen so quickly. I've never seen any of these face-on for five minutes or so, so you can actually study them and work out pictures. It's always quick. It was just black, no detail. Black. All black. Everything. And it was male – just feelings…

'So I just walked through, put the carrycot on the table, unloaded whatever it was I was unloading on the table, picked up the carrycot, very calmly walked back out and waited in the barn for Bill. It was snowing outside – it was very cold. Rebecca was tiny. The last thing you're thinking about when you've got two kids and stuff to unload is spooky things, but there was no way I was going back into that hallway.'

*

It was as if that apparition had breached some invisible wall. From that moment on, the terror in the house grew rapidly worse.

Chapter 6

The flight from the house was like a surreal dream. Liz's vision of the black figure was the final straw. Reality had collapsed around them and all they remember was the thunder of blood in their ears and an assortment of images that seemed to make no sense: clothes being stuffed into suitcases, hedges passing the car window in a blur of green and gold, the sky, the hills, other traffic. Their hearts were beating out the rhythm of their madness and even when some comprehension of their surroundings returned, they still had to face the paranoia and anxiety that *it* was after them, screaming at their heels, trying to drag them back, keeping them prisoners forever.

Eventually they pulled over into a layby and hugged each other as they searched deep within themselves for strength. There were tears and anger, hopelessness and fear. Behind them, the children sat quietly.

In the lull that followed the emotional outburst, Bill murmured, 'I can't believe what's happened to our lives. Sometimes I feel like I'm going mad. All those rules that can build a structure for your life… what can and can't happen… they're not there anymore. It's just chaos. I never thought I could be so terrified *all* of the time, just waiting for something to happen.'

'Why is it happening to us, Bill? What have we done? It never happened to Bridget Buscombe like this.'

He shook his head.

'And what is it?' There was desperation in her question that frightened him.

'You know I've never been much of a one for religion…' he began, before his words stumbled. 'It's not just ghosts, you know that. You've *felt* it. There's something evil in that house, Liz. I'm pretty sure it wants to destroy us.' He paused, and then added, 'And I think it wants our souls. That sounds melodramatic, but I really believe it.'

‘Then why didn’t the exorcisms work?’ Liz asked tearfully.

‘Perhaps it was just too strong.’

Liz glanced into the back seat at the children. ‘Thank God it’s not affecting them.’

‘If only we could just run away from it. Keep driving and driving until there are so many miles between us and the house we don’t have to think about it.’ Bill stared blankly out of the windscreen. ‘But we can’t do that. We’ve got no money – it’s already seen to that. We can’t afford to stay anywhere. We can’t get rehoused. We’ve got to keep strong… keep on going for the children’s sake. We can’t just live out of a car. We’re trapped.’ He bit his lip until he tasted blood.

‘The worst thing is all these people we turn to for help,’ Liz said. ‘They’re talking about a completely different world that I can’t understand, but we’ve got no choice but to believe them. When I hear them speak, I feel like I’m being grabbed by the arms and spun round. They make me dizzy with their talk of psychic walls and demonic entities. But we can’t afford *not* to believe them. God, I feel so… desperate.’

‘I never thought we’d use that word, but you’re right. We’re desperate. Sometimes I think we’re down to a battle for survival.’

Liz grabbed Bill’s hand and squeezed it tightly. ‘We’re doing it for the children,’ she said. ‘That’s our focus. Whatever happens… however bad it gets… it’s for them.’

Bill looked back at Ben and Rebecca’s faces, but all he could see was through them, across the fields and trees and the hills, to a dark, empty house, silently summoning them back.

*

They spoke for a while longer about the black figure Liz had seen and her feeling that the evil had finally broken through in the house. Then Liz called her mother and asked if they could stay for a while. Although Mrs Sanders couldn’t grasp the fears they were trying to express, she welcomed them with open arms. They drove to Cowbridge in silence, and outside the house decided to stay as long as they could without becoming a burden.

While they were there, they saw the local vicar and prayed together for some release. It was becoming apparent to both of them that religion was the only thing they could count on for support.

Liz's mother lived over a shoe shop. One day Liz started chatting to one of the assistants. She mentioned the problems they had had at Heol Fanog; in her weary, broken state she didn't care if people believed her or not. The assistant asked her if she had heard of Reverend Arthur Neil, an evangelist who had written several books on exorcism.

That afternoon Liz called the Evangelical Training College in Bridgend to get his number. Mr Neil was in his late seventies and was caring for a wife with cancer, which he said prevented him from helping personally. However, he gave Liz the number of a colleague, Davis Holmwood, a Baptist minister who lived and worked in their area.

Bill called him that night and explained the problem. As they were talking, the line began to crackle and break up. 'Just interference,' Bill said, but Mr Holwood disagreed. 'The enemy will do anything to stop this conversation taking place,' he said.

Bill was sure it was simply a faulty line, but he was glad the Reverend was listening and planning to help. Over the next few days they had several other conversations about Heol Fanog and then he visited the Riches in Cowbridge to talk over his approach to the exorcism. Throughout that time, Mr Holmwood was fasting in preparation for a visit to the house, and when he felt he was ready he promised to fix a date.

*

In the meantime, Bill phoned Laurence to see how he was getting on. They had spoken several times since his son had moved into the boarding house, and on those occasions Laurence had been as sullen as always. That evening however there was such a transformation that Bill couldn't believe it. Laurence was laughing and joking. In fact, he sounded exactly like the boy who first moved into Heol Fanog.

As the conversation progressed, Laurence said suddenly, 'You did the right thing, Dad. Getting me out of that house. I don't want to talk about what happened there, but... Anyway, I'm better now. I'm fine. I feel like a weight's been taken off my shoulders.'

They spoke some more and when Bill finally put the phone down, he felt like crying. It was their first victory, and it had been the most important one.

When he went back into Liz, he said simply, 'Laurence has been saved.'

*

Bill, Liz and the children were staying in the two top rooms of her mother's house. Though they were away from Heol Fanog and its black atmosphere, things still did not seem wholly *right*. They couldn't put their finger on what it was exactly – a hangover from their previous anxiety, depression perhaps – but it was certainly there, and over the previous few months they had learned to trust their feelings.

What had concerned them so much in Heol Fanog was how mundane things were amplified into the range of terrifying: simple sounds or smells or fleeting glimpses, which taken in isolation could be easily dismissed by a third party. No one truly understood how a cold chill in a warm room could manufacture an overpowering fear. And that was how it became in Cowbridge.

The pool of water that appeared one day on the bathroom floor was not inherently frightening. Yet Bill and Liz's senses were heightened and ready for anything even slightly out of the normal; there was no explanation for it.

It wasn't urine or orange juice from the children. No one had even been in the room between the time it wasn't there and the time it was. Bill checked the ceiling above to see if it could have leaked through the roof, from a water tank or a pipe; there was no likely source, no sign of discoloration on the white ceiling where the water would have dripped through. They mopped it up and tried to discount it, but at that stage, every odd thing had significance.

The next day it appeared again. The same spot, same size; once more, no cause. Bill and Liz were by this time used to thorough checking to eliminate every possible explanation, until they were only left with the impossible. It was not a phenomenon that had happened in Heol Fanog. They were puzzled, but they had long since given up trying to read any meaning into the inexplicable occurrences that assailed them.

The water wasn't the only thing. A few days after they had moved into Cowbridge, Liz's mother spotted a strange pendant, without its chain, on the living room floor. It was about half an inch long, oval and black-green with age – it seemed ancient. It was just possible to make out a faint Egyptian design. It wasn't hers and it hadn't been there before, so she presumed Liz must have dropped it. She picked it up and showed it to Bill and Liz when they came in later. The Riches hadn't seen it before either and no one else had been in the room.

Bill picked it up and then leapt back with a cry, dropping the pendant instantly. His fingers had been burnt by a short, sharp shock, like a bolt of electricity. They scooped the pendant on to a newspaper and took it outside where they smashed it to pieces with a hammer.

By then they were quite sure. Whatever was in Heol Fanog had followed them, albeit in a weakened form.

*

Liz's testimony: 'The pools of water just started appearing. My mother's house doesn't leak. There are no taps upstairs, but these pools of water were appearing. That really frightened me, because it was real. I couldn't say, "No!" because it was there.

'All the time I was staying in Cowbridge, I would go out for walks with the children. I felt so peculiar. Everyone else was going on with their lives. They were doing the shopping, going for their lunch, doing whatever they were doing, and there was I… bloody hell! What was I doing?! In the end you become apart from people because you know you can't talk to them about it. And I don't like talking to people much about the weather and things – there's not much point. Even my older brother, who's read about the occult, can't handle it – it's happening too close to home. So the water thing just happened at my mother's. I can't remember it happening here. If it happened here I'd just put it down to the kids. But it almost, like, followed us and that really freaked me out. I didn't like that.

'The pendant was spooky too. It really shocked Bill when he picked it up and dropped it. There was no one else who could have been in the house and left it there. It was almost like it had appeared there for us to find. And the Egyptian design was so strange, with what happened to us in Egypt. And what Bill was to see a few months later…'

*

While they were away, Bill had to return to Heol Fanog every day to feed the five goats and their cat. The drive to the house always left him nervous and shaking. As he drew near to Heol Fanog, he felt the tension sweep over him. The roads seemed to be filled with danger, and he became acutely aware he was driving a car with no tax, insurance or MOT because they couldn't afford to pay for them.

The brooding presence was there the moment he stepped through the door and the only way he could cope with it was by switching his mind off and going through his chores by rote. Each day when he left his only thought was that he had survived.

*

The Riches couldn't stay with Liz's mother indefinitely, so they reluctantly returned to Heol Fanog in June 1991. The fear was there immediately.

David Holmwood finally felt ready to visit the house and Bill met him in Brecon while Liz took the children out for the day. He was a heavily built man, over six feet tall, aged about fifty-five. He was accompanied by a large, short American woman of about forty who, with her dark hair and swarthy skin, looked imposing. Anita Dick was a reformed Satanist who had been exorcized by Arthur Neil. She had accompanied David Holmwood the first time he had met the Riches in Cowbridge.

The house seemed worse for having been empty for so long. There was no electricity and the garden was overgrown with long, yellow grass. There was a dead bird in the living room and another in the kitchen because Bill had left the window open for the cat to get in and out. The sense of menace was almost tangible.

All David Holmwood and Anita Dick wanted to do was walk around the house and gardens to get the feel of the place.

*

Bill's testimony: 'Every time we had somebody in the house I thought they were going to call me a fool. They were going to say, "Well, we can't find anything. It's all in your mind. It's all in your imagination. It's not happening. It can't be happening." But, no. Quite the opposite. Everybody found something.

'By this time you would have thought that we would have plenty of knowledge of these people – "Wake up, man. They're all a load of bloody nutcases" – but we didn't, because we were still aware of the fact that there was *the problem*. The problem was still there so we had to get some help from somewhere. There was a part of me saying, "I'm not going to be beaten by this. I won't be beaten by this! Whatever it is… I don't understand it… but I don't see why it should kick us out of what could be a lovely home."

'There was one night where David and Anita interrogated us for hours, until about two in the morning. Afterwards they drove back from Cowbridge to Merthyr and as they did so this huge owl smashed into the windscreen. It didn't break it, but it just exploded and there was blood everywhere. Anita predicted it was some act of

Satan out to stop them. When people start saying things like that to me, I say, "Well it might or might not be.""

*

Liz returned to Cowbridge with the children, and David Holmwood and Anita Dick appeared in July 1991. They had spent days fasting and praying and when Bill met them in Brecon they told him they needed to prepare before entering the house. Bill sat in the back of their car while they bowed their heads and prayed for protection. When they had finished, Bill climbed back into his own car and led the way.

Along the journey, Bill repeatedly checked in his rear view mirror to ensure they were behind him, but when he drew up outside the house there was no sign of them. Bill waited nervously, occasionally stepping out into the road to listen for the sound of an engine, but the lane was too sinuous; it was impossible to tell what had happened to them. They arrived ten minutes later, looking pale and shaken.

Bill helped them out of the car, frantically asking what had happened. They told him 'the Enemy' had attacked them in the car. It had gone off the road and they had struggled with him there, praying and calling on him to leave Bill alone.

Bill looked terrified, but David Holmwood merely smiled and told him it was already over; they had won the fight, the Enemy was gone and there was nothing left for them to do.

Having seen no sign of the struggle, Bill found it hard to believe, but when he stepped through the gates to the property, he immediately recognized a change in the atmosphere. Once more it had the lovely tranquillity that had first attracted him to the place.

There was no electricity, and yet another dead bird inside, but the house, too, seemed at peace. David and Anita told Bill it was important to ensure the house was free of all evil influence, and that involved clearing out anything that might attract "evil presence".

The first thing David saw was one of Bill's surreal paintings, which featured an eye as its central image. It was a striking piece of work, but David insisted it felt evil; anything like that, David said, could act as a channel to bring further evil into the house. The painting had to go.

Bill was devastated. His head was swimming from what David said had happened in the car, and although he was filled with hope that all the torment of Heol Fanog was over, he was loath to rid himself of a unique creation he had slaved over for days, something that was *him*. David insisted and Bill felt too destabilized to resist. He had put all his faith in David to save them and the only way he could do that was to accept everything he said implicitly. Depressively, he helped carry the painting out to David's car.

But it didn't end there. David and Anita systematically went through the house, delving into all of Bill and Liz's possessions, removing everything which they felt could be a focus for the Enemy. Bill watched blankly as some of his best-loved belongings were heaped into a washing basket and then loaded into David's car: another painting, some antique brass incense burners from Burma, a life-size papier mache figure of a man, nearly all of Bill's books, a good library he had built up over the years for reference, including books on ancient Spanish, Buddhism and others which had detailed the paranormal. The removal took the rest of the day, and David and Anita stopped only when they felt nothing remained that could be a focus for evil. Barely able to hide his sadness, Bill enquired what would happen to all his things. David told him they would be burnt, including his paintings.

Just before they left, Bill asked Anita what had occurred in the car and how they knew it was over. She said they heard a voice that could only have come from God. It said: 'It is finished.' Before departing they opened all the windows in the house because 'any departing entities can leave by smashing glass'.

Bill locked the house and returned to Cowbridge where he told Liz what had happened. His hope that David Holmwood had brought about an ending to their troubles was tempered by the loss of all his possessions. The next day they returned to the house with

Bill and Liz's mothers and cleaned it from top to bottom in preparation for their return. So they would have some electricity for the vacuum cleaner Bill went to feed the new token meter installed by Swalec after his complaints about the power drain; his tokens were swallowed up rapidly.

*

Although Bill and Liz never felt the 'horror thing' over the next few months, they were still convinced something was there. The sensation of being watched was always present, although it seemed weaker, as if the watcher had moved into the background for a while. Every time they had an unusual sensation, they telephoned David for prayers; he had become an anchor in their lives, one of the few people who had believed in the madness and who seemed to have had success in dealing with it.

For his part, David Holmwood remained in regular contact with them. He phoned them once a week and visited once a fortnight for prayers and the laying on of hands. After a while, the Riches decided to become Baptists.

*

Liz's testimony: 'I was so looking forward to being baptized, to totally becoming Jesus's and to an end of the craziness. I was convinced that after baptism it would all end. The service was wonderful. I remember having to give my testimony, but I broke down and Bill took over. The atmosphere was electric in church. I felt the presence of the Holy Spirit had entered us. But after the baptism everything got worse.'

*

The testimony of David Holmwood, Baptist minister: 'I look on myself as a GP in spiritual terms. It's a learning thing and I'm constantly using everything I've learnt. I've been a Christian since I was fifteen and the moment I decided that was what I was going to be, I felt a feeling like electricity, which has never left me. The same thing has happened to my own son.

'After Bill contacted me, I went up there with Anita Dick to check out how valid the story was. The place was certainly dark in spiritual terms. There was a sense – an atmosphere – you could pick up when walking around. Some houses are obviously light and airy, but that place wasn't. Bill and Liz were in an obvious panic and they had an extreme desire for help, something they could depend on in terms of sincerity and down-to-earthness, if you can use that term in connection with that place.

'I took a lot of notes. I was previously an electrical engineer and factory manager, so I was quite methodical in my approach. I wrote down their story to look for links which might have been behind what was happening, things which my own mind queried and wanted to start probing. One of the senses we don't use in this spiritual realm is the sense of feeling – you can "feel" things in an emotional way. I went through Liz's personal history and then Bill's personal history, dealing with this is a logical manner and seeking to find out where the doors into the spiritual had been opened. In my eyes, for this to happen, there must be somewhere where someone has opened themselves up to the spiritual dimension. In Bill's life, I felt there where several occasions when he could have crossed over or come close. For instance, when he used to live with that chap Saunders of the witches.

'It took a month of visits, but when you have to see a change in someone, you have to make a personal commitment. There was one evening when I was down in Cowbridge at Liz's mother's home. We were all sitting on the veranda at about 11 p.m., talking intently. There was a feeling… a tremendous sense of satanic power in the air. You could certainly feel it… tremendously strong. Then suddenly there was a moment of respite – a lull in the attack – and I instantly said to Bill, "Will you ask Jesus Christ into your heart?" He said, "Yes, please." And we prayed a prayer with Bill and then we did the same with Liz and at that moment they became Christians. And then the force of power started up again, but it was too late and that was when the battle was won.

'Following that, all sorts of things were happening in the house, so I arranged to take Anita there and meet Bill. You have to do this kind of thing in pairs, so that the full power of force of whatever you're up against isn't directed at an individual. It was in Luke 10, I think, where Jesus sent them out in pairs to expel demons. Before going into the house we prayed on the hillside for two and half hours.

'Then we set off for the house, following Bill, who was driving ahead. We were only about half a mile away when I suddenly felt a tremendous force on my chest, as if someone was trying to crush me. I stopped the car because I thought I was going to pass out. It felt like a band had been fastened around my chest. I asked Anita to pray with me until the force finally went. As we continued on our way, I felt the battle for the house had really been won on the hillside. When we got to the house, whatever had been there had gone.

'Bill had a collection of books and I had to take away anything that gave permission for the spirits to be there. I took away fifty-four books – I counted them – and left them overnight in the car. The next day I asked my son Jon, who was home from university, if he would help me unload this stuff. I took the car round the back of the cottage where we lived and prepared to offload the books in the centre of the back garden so we could burn them. As Jon took the first book out of the back of the car, he got a sudden electric shock. "Now you know what we're up against," I said. It made him aware that the dimension we were dealing with was very powerful. We needed protection from it. We also heard a sound in the air, like a giant cat. We burnt the books and drawings and smashed up the crystals. One of the paintings had an eye in it, which is a freemasonry symbol. Freemasonry lets the dark side of evil forces through. Not everybody is affected, of course, but some people are susceptible, for power, for wanting to feel good. It is a terrific driving force, but not human. Symbols are the things we look at because they can be a doorway into another world. We very much go by sense, feeling the way as we go, but my maxim on that occasion was: if in doubt, throw it out. Some of the books mentioned ley lines. There was another called *Satanic Rites of the High Priests*. These doorways had to be closed off.

‘Why did I do this? Just out of experience. There are two stories I can tell to support it, which concern a friend of mine who was a chaplain at Hackney Hospital. I was called in to a situation by a lady who’s own vicar wasn’t available. I went round to see her and she was very frightened by something in her room. She didn’t know what it was, but I gave her a text of scripture and we prayed, as is common in these circumstances. As I went out and put my hand on the Yale lock to leave, there was a voice in my head which said, “Go back into the room and pray for the family.”

‘As I walked back into that room, she screamed out for help and grabbed my hand. Across the room came a wind, freezing cold, straight towards me. It was like being in the middle of a storm. I had never experienced anything like this before. I just raised my right hand and said, “In the name of the Lord Jesus, I command you to go from this place.” It took me fifteen to twenty minutes calling on the name of Jesus Christ, the power and the blood of Jesus Christ, to get that thing to go.

‘I immediately phoned up Roger, the chaplain at Hackney Hospital, and asked him to come and help me. When he arrived, he said to the woman, “Is there anything in this room that disturbs you?” She pointed to a picture and he turned it to the wall. Then he asked her if there was anything which had come back from overseas. She said there was a carved head which an uncle had brought back from Africa. It was in the cellar. Roger is a big man and not scared of anything so he went down there and had a look around, but he couldn’t find it. He returned and told her if she could find it the next day, she should burn it. And she did.

‘The following Wednesday we went back and had a small Communion service. When we walked in, the whole oppression in the place had gone. It was light and sunny. We realized the battle had been won. I prayed for guardian angels to look over the place. It worked – whatever had been there didn’t come back.

‘The other story concerned a nurse at Hackney Hospital. She was a Malaysian, like a lot of nurses there, and she went to Roger to convert. But she was very frightened of an amulet given her by a priest in her home country. In fact, it terrified her so much she was scared to touch it. Priscilla, Roger's wife, took it off her. It was a gold amulet. Roger took it away, walked around, and when he got home at midnight he went out to the front of the house and bashed it with a hammer. But however much he tried he couldn't destroy it, so he dropped it down the nearest storm drain.

'Although the things I am talking about sound uncanny – weird – they are nevertheless real. These kind of things are all possible doorways. If they have been prayed over and committed to that purpose, they become a doorway, with spirits having a permission to come through.

'Bill and Liz became church members and were baptized. I have seen them regularly over the last four years. It moves you. They are full of grace and truth. Something happened there that completely transformed their lives. All I can say is, Jesus did it.'

*

Bill's testimony: 'On that day when they claimed to have fought the Enemy in the car, David came into the house, saw a painting with an eye that I had done. Didn't like it. That had to go. Various pieces of antique brass from Burma, they had to go. I had a very good library which featured a certain amount of occult books, because I was interested in lots of things, from Buddhism to ancient Spanish, and they were there for reference. They had to go.

'They were talking away, out of the house, everything that they believed could be a focus for evil. And again I believed them. Books that cost me £20, £25, but they could have been a focus for evil. Likewise, my great painting with the eye went to be burnt, along with my books. And some of the old brass that I had grown quite attached to.

'Just before they left I asked Anita what had happened. I said, "Why aren't you going anything in the house like all the others?" She said, "Because it all happened in the car. We heard this voice and it could only have come from God. It said, "It is finished". And that's why we knew, when we got to the house, that there was nothing to do inside the house, apart from taking from it what we thought could be a focus for evil."

'When I drove to Cowbridge, I felt drained and my mind was whirling. I didn't know *what* to tell Liz. But this was the time in our minds that we thought it had really finished.'

*

It was at that time that Bill began to re-experience a growing desperation about his painting, the feeling of 'Do it now or you will never get the chance to do it again.' He didn't know if it was a regressive fatalism brought on by the mood of the house over the previous weeks, or a selfish impulse to hold on to what was essentially his in the face of all sorts of pressures – a child, money worries, the house – but it was undoubtedly driving him into the studio more and more to stand before that giant canvas.

He had spent too long away from his masterpiece, but gradually it began to take shape. There was a tangle of tubes entrapping the bleeding heart, and a smattering of tears, in dusky pinks and love-lorn blues; Bill was surprised to feel palpable sadness about the work, which he hadn't envisaged when the idea first came to him. He had already thought of a title taken from one of his favourite poems, by the poet Maurice Maeterlinck: 'The Voice of Mankind is Still and Sadness Hangs Over All.'

Although their relationship was solid, Bill had opted to sleep in another room so he could work late and go to bed without disturbing anyone. Liz stayed in the main bedroom and got up to check on the children if they were disturbed during the night. About six months after David Holmwood had had his victory, Liz began to complain of trouble sleeping because their cat was under the bed during the night and 'snoring' so loudly it woke her. Normally exhausted after a day looking after the children, she didn't have the energy to get out of bed and move the cat so she forced herself to go back to sleep.

This went on for a week before Liz decided she had had enough. At 3 a.m. on the seventh night, bleary-eyed and weary, she swung over the edge of the bed and peered underneath; the cat's snoring was so loud it seemed like a traction engine. In the dark of the room, she couldn't see the cat anywhere, so angrily she clambered out of bed and switched on the light.

She returned to the bed, dropped to her knees and looked under it. The cat wasn't there.

Curiously, Liz began to search around the room. Under the chest of drawers. In the wardrobe. The cat wasn't in the room at all, but the snoring was as loud as ever. Suddenly all the other phenomena that had plagued them over months came rushing back and Liz dropped nervously on to the edge of the bed. She forced herself to focus on the snoring. It didn't really sound like cat at all, did it? Not a nice, little domestic puss. Something much, much bigger - a lion, or a tiger.

She glanced around, searching for its source. Slowly, it dawned on her that it wasn't in the room at all. Her gaze trailed across the floor, over the chest of drawers, the chair, the head of the bed, to the window. That was where it was coming from.

Outside the window.

That familiar tingle of fear came back into her stomach. Liz stood up, resting the outside of her knee against the bed for support. The curtains were drawn, although there was a tiny crack between them. Anxiously, she tried to peer through, but it was impossible to see anything other than the dark night.

'Draw them back. Have a look. Don't be silly,' she told herself. Other people might have instantly found a rational explanation for the sound, but having lived in an irrational world for so long, Liz's options were much greater, and much more frightening.

She took a step forward.

As she did so, the storing stopped a notch. It was as if whatever was outside the window had seen her approach and had taken a step back. Liz took another step; the snoring diminished further. Buoyed by this, Liz strode forward and flung the curtains back.

The cloudless night was impenetrable and with the bedroom light on, it was impossible to pick anything out of the gloom. Yet Liz didn't want to switch it off; the darkness was best outside. All she could tell was that nothing was moving.

Deciding to wake Bill to tell him about it, she took a step back. The snoring grew louder. Like it was advancing. Liz turned and ran from the room, down the landing to Bill's studio where he was still painting. He hated being disturbed when he was working, but he could see the fear in Liz's face. She led him back along the landing and into the bedroom. The room was silent.

Bill glanced at her questioningly and Liz burst into tears. 'It was here, Bill. It was! You believe me, don't you?'

He took her into his arms and gave her a hug, all the time listening for any sound. 'Of course I believe you,' he whispered.

In the double bed next to where Liz had been, Rebecca was still sleeping. Bill led Liz on to the landing, where they could talk without disturbing their daughter.

'It sounded like an animal, Bill. Just outside the window. Like it was watching… waiting for a chance to come in. All those nights I thought it was the cat under the bed. And it wasn't, it was there outside. This is something new, Bill. What's here now?'

'Perhaps it was just a cat outside. Or a bird in the loft. Or something.' Even then, after everything that had happened, he tried to hold on to some kind of rationality.

'Sure,' Liz said. There was a trace of bitterness and irony in her voice. 'You'll look tomorrow?'

'Of course I will.'

It was forcing Liz to question her own sanity. Previously, everything had been experienced by both of them. Suddenly she felt so alone, so tormented, like it was trying to make Bill ask if she had imagined it. But he had seen and heard enough over the months not to do that. 'It's after me. Why me?' she kept repeating. And then she'd ask Bill once again if he believed her, seeking the reassurance she needed to continue.

Although Bill hadn't heard the 'snoring', he sensed Liz's deep dread. He returned to his studio while Liz and Rebecca moved into another room. Twice more he returned to the bedroom to check and on the third time he heard it. It *was* like they were under attack and each new wave brought a different and more terrifying peril.

*

The next day Liz's father came round and with Bill scrambled through the loft, searching for any cats or birds. There was no sign anything had been in there. Her father was baffled by Liz's description of the sound; it didn't sound like any animal he knew. And there was nowhere outside the window for any animal to perch. 'Unless it was a flying cat,' he joked.

The snoring sound was there the next night and the next. After a month of broken sleep and terrible dreams about what was outside the window, they felt their nerves had been tightened to breaking point.

They had put off calling David Holmwood for as long as they could. They didn't want to keep disturbing him about every single thing that happened in Heol Fanog, especially when it was just a sound, but at that point Liz could take no more.

Mr Holmwood understood immediately. 'It has been here too,' he said flatly.

He told Bill that when his son had taken Bill's possessions into the back garden to burn them, he had been assailed by the snoring noise. It seemed to be all around him, although there was no physical presence. David Holmwood described whatever was making the snoring noise as a 'Spirit of the Air' and said had only left his son alone when he had started to pray.

Bill and David Holmwood prayed on the phone for deliverance from the threatening spirit and that night Liz had her first unbroken sleep for a month. They never heard the sound again.

*

Liz's testimony: 'The worst actual things that happened on the psychic, spiritual level, for me, were the snoring and the water. These were physical things and I couldn't pretend they weren't happening. That's what got to me. I shut everything out – all the ghosts, and the sounds and the smells and the feelings. But that, the snoring, happened in the end bedroom. Now, shit, that really frightened me, because for over a week I'd been sleeping with it and the cat wasn't even there.'

Chapter 7

Like all good mystery stories, the clues began to present themselves over time. Some were red herrings, some were half-truths, some seemed to point in one direction and some in another. But after a while certain things began to gel, some pieces of information supported others and there was a chance for the Riches to begin to build some kind of picture. It was hazy, but after being trapped in the dark of not knowing anything, every new revelation came as a blinding light. The question was simply: what made Heol Fanog such a terrible place? The evidence came from many sources: history books, aged texts buried in the local library, village gossip, rumour and hear say, experts and helpful but knowledgeable amateurs.

As much information as possible was the key. The Riches knew that when dealing with the paranormal they would never identify a definite cause for their misfortune. There were no simple lines of cause and effect laid down by science, and so there would be no pat answers, just possibilities. And the only guidelines Bill and Liz could follow were folklore, occult and religious beliefs.

Received knowledge says ghosts are trapped spirits of people in torment at the time they died. There are plenty of other theories too, but the 'suffering departed' is common currency and that was the theory the Riches concentrated on to begin with. A local historian had provided them with what was known about the history of the area, and the Riches did their own investigations among the local hill farmers and close neighbours who had accounts passed down through the generations.

The area around Heol Fanog is steeped in stories of blood and murder. The main documented case dates back to 1848 when Thomas Edwards, a 23-year-old resident farm worker with the Powell family, attacked James Griffiths, an 18-year-old employed on a casual, short-term basis. Edwards bludgeoned Griffiths in the back of the head with an axe and buried the body in a muck heap at the farm where they both worked, Cwm Gwdi, just down the valley from Heol Fanog.

Details of the background to the murder are sketchy, as could be expected from a rural murder that took place long before the turn of the century. There is a lot of local knowledge about the crime, but folk memory gets garbled and it was difficult for the Riches to sift what little hard facts there are from the colourful additions made over the years. Local historians have done a lot of work on the case, however, establishing that Edwards was hanged in Brecon and that shortly before the crime he had asked his employer, John Powell, for an advance on his wages because the annual fair day was approaching and he wanted a new coat.

The implication is that Edwards attacked Griffiths for money, although there is no evidence of this. Local folklore says the murder happened following an argument about the farmer's daughter, whom Edwards and Griffiths both loved. Edwards is buried at the nearby Llanhamlach Church.

Although the body was found at Cwm Gwdi, there is nothing to say the murder took place there. Bill Rich was told the murder actually happened in the garden of Heol Fanog, near the old manor house, and the body was dumped at Cwm Gwdi so as not to attract attention to the property. Why? It was a question that had puzzled the locals for many years. Just before the end, Bill would be told a possible explanation from the strangest source of all.

There is a local story of a gypsy murdered at an old bridge over a small stream, just a stone's throw from Heol Fanog. Many nearby residents won't cross the bridge at night. A further story passed down by word of mouth concerns a murder in a cowshed at Blaen Gwdi, another farm near to Heol Fanog. The farmer was killed by his wife, who blamed a young, simple farm worker. Her accusation sent him to the gallows. It is possible this murder may be a garbled version of the Cwm Gwdi murder, but all go to show that the area immediately around Heol Fanog has a long-standing reputation for death and brutality.

Another folk tale, which may have some bearing, involves a man sent to the gallows unjustly. It is confused with the story of a local highwayman, but, once again, according to folklore the condemned man was trying to loosen the noose around his neck when then warder knocked his hands away. The gathered crowd went wild with anger and the warder couldn't walk the streets for months after for fear of his own life.

There were rumours of black magic surrounding many of the murders. Brecon has a long-standing history of witchcraft, with many powerful covens dating back to the Middle Ages. Stories of their dark deeds play powerfully in the collective unconscious of the town and many tales of rituals continue to this day. At first glance, hints of ancient witchcraft ceremonies at Heol Fanog seem to fit the pattern being created, yet it would continue the historic injustice to Britain's first religion to carry through with this superficial train of thinking.

*

The testimony of Gil August, doctor of anthropology, Builth Wells: 'I'm an anthropologist working to show a link between Palaeolithic and Neolithic belief structures, particularly the belief in a horned god, which we pick up in the eleventh and twelfth centuries as witchcraft. It's hard to follow up rumours of covens today because they are flimsy and almost verging on urban legends. Whenever something strange happens, the Baptists and Methodists always say there must have been witches involved. What they are really talking about are Satanists. Satanists are not witches. Satanists are Christians because Satan is a Christian concept. This kind of confusion has been going on for centuries. Witches weren't evil. They had an extremely high moral structure. To an actual practicing witch, life was precious because it was a religion linked to nature and the cycles of nature. When a witch saw a child, they didn't want to sacrifice it – in the child they saw the promise of continuance which they saw in nature. Witchcraft is derivative of the Anglo-Saxon term wiccae, which means wisdom. It referred to the person in the village with knowledge. Witches were revered. In the fifteenth and sixteenth century, you would go to a witch's grave to make the most solemn vow.'

*

Gossip, rumours and wild tales are rife in a town like Brecon; one such tale which deserves mention concerns the mother of the current owner of Heol Fanog, Phil Holbourn. It is regularly told by the locals, but because of Mr Holbourn's high standing in the community, no one would repeat it on record. Shortly before she died, and while she was still living in Heol Fanog, his mother, Mrs Marion Holbourn, became terrified of some awful supernatural presence in the house, the story goes. So frightened, in fact, that she insisted the vicar and entire choir of the local church, St David's, come to the house to carry out an exorcism. Mrs Holbourn was convinced only such a weight of people would maximize the force for good needed to defeat whatever dark force had moved into her home. Mrs Holbourn lived in the house in the late fifties through to the early sixties and, according to some people in the town old enough to remember, the vicar and choir trooped up to Heol Fanog on foot reciting blessings in a procession so bizarre it stuck in the minds of all who saw it. The echoes with the case of Bill and Liz Rich are eerie to say the least.

*

Phil Holbourn, owner of Heol Fanog, recollected things differently: 'If my mother arranged anything like that, I can't recall it. She used to have all sorts of people going to visit her at various times. I know she did once have a service up there because she was trying to create a fragrant garden for the blind, so perhaps some people have got their wires crossed.

'I'm not aware of anything strange happening in Heol Fanog. None of the previous residents have said anything to me.'

*

The spiritualists were the first to link the phenomena in some way to ley lines. According to several people who visited Heol Fanog, the property is criss-crossed with leys; in fact, the confluence of so many lines makes the property particularly unusual to those who study leys and it has attracted a great deal of interest from scholars and dowsers particularly interested in this debate.

The fact that Heol Fanog is notable for two separate areas of unexplained phenomena is certainly worth explaining. All the theories on ley lines are too complicated to examine in detail here, but a crash course in the study of ley lines can provide enough of a springboard for further examination.

Most people have heard of ley lines. The term was coined in 1921 by Alfred Watkins, a respected Hertfordshire brewer, who had a moment of startling lucidity on a country walk when he noticed a strange pattern in the landscape. Ancient standing stones, old churches and monuments, manmade hills, crossroads and other features seemed strangely aligned. His further research showed these straight lines were all over the country, with stone circles and Neolithic mounds providing the most important markers; many churches and later monuments fit the bill because they were built on the site of ancient buildings or earthworks. Watkins assumed the leys were ancient trading routes, but that hypothesis has since been discarded.

In its place are a whole host of theories from the canny to the crackpot, covering the spectrum from the scientific to the spiritual: spirit paths, routes for the dead to find the afterlife; road markers for UFOs; funeral tracks for the ancients. Adding fuel to the debate is the fact that dowsers can locate and track leys in the same way they can find underground water, mineral deposits and archaeological artefacts.

This has led to a theory of an earth force, to which the dowsers are responding. Earth energy, electromagnetic fields, geopathic stress – different names have been bandied around as the dowsers grapple with a subject that seems to resist scientific interpretation. Dowsers themselves are divided on the matter: rationalists struggle to give it pseudoscientific gloss, while those on the more spiritual side have an almost religious acceptance of energy fields, which cannot be mapped to the satisfaction of scientists. Crazy or not, it's a simple fact that three dowsers taken independently to the same spot will get the same result.

Many of these invisible channels of energy link prehistoric sites. The ancient Chinese were strong believers in the earth force, which they christened *lung mei* (paths of the dragon), an energy which could be split up into two kinds, yin and yang or male and female. They believed it was imperative that important buildings were sited where there was a proper balance of yin and yang and the art of this eventually became *feng shui* (wind and water) – it was practiced by professional geomancers.

For more than half a century dowsers have been talking about the parlous effect of black streams or negative leys. They are, according to the believers, lines where the earth is out of balance. They have been linked with mental illness and various physical illnesses like cancer and epilepsy in those who live above them. Dowsers can treat black streams in many ways: by hammering metal rods into the earth to change the energy flow like a large scale version of acupuncture, with crystals, or with machines known as Raditechs which, again, are supposed to rebalance the energy.

There's no 'proof' that the energy is there, but there's plenty of testimonies from people who have lived above black streams and who have experiences of before and after treatment. Of course, the sceptics will always say it was all in the mind in the first place, and that the mind simply responded to something being done, not *what* was done. That's far too glib a response to the weight of evidence the dowsers have presented to support their case.

Many other strange phenomena appear to be linked to ley lines. A good number of UFO sightings have been made above particularly strong leys, which may be linked to reports of 'earth lights', strange globes of colour that act like ball lightning and which have been attributed to an electromagnetic by-product of geopathic stress along the lines. There are other, darker, stories too.

Ley lines had been known by tradition for years as the 'old straight tracks' long before Watkins brought the understanding of them into the twentieth century. And interweaved with this was the local folklore of spirit paths, with tales of scared villagers claiming they had witnessed the recently departed walking along them to the other side. It is a fact that many historically haunted sites are located on leys, and dowsers have their own peculiar mythology which links the earth energy at focal points to apparitions. It would be interesting to see a study of the connection between leys and haunted houses; the verbal evidence from dowsers over the years is overwhelming. Perhaps, as some of the dowsers on the spiritual wing believe, the energy is so powerful it traps the spirits and draws in other 'non-human entities' to feed on it. Or perhaps the energy, whatever it is, is simply so powerful it affects the chemical balances and electric firings of the human brain. Who knows? But it is here that the link between Heol Fanog and the leys becomes interesting. For not only does Heol Fanog seem to be the most supernaturally afflicted house in Britain, it is also at a nexus of the most potently negative earth energy.

*

Dickie Dodds became a dowser in 1987, when he retired and moved into a new house. He and his wife were beset by a succession of ailments that kept recurring despite numerous trips to the doctor. Yet, miraculously, the couple found they felt better whenever they spent a night in London, away from their Bedfordshire home. After a while, someone mentioned the concept of black streams to him and he called in a dowser, who told him there was an underground river flowing beneath his property. That helped create the black stream or negative ley. Dodds was so impressed with the dowser's results he taught himself to dowse and has since been helping people around the country. He visited Heol Fanog is early June 1995 after hearing reports of the Rich family's difficulties.

*

The testimony of Dickie Dodds, dowser: 'Dowsers use several different names for these phenomena, but black streams is one of the common ones. It is radiation from the earth which, when passing through running water, has its frequency altered so that it is harmful to people. My wife got cancer after lying in a bed over one of these lines, as did the woman who moved into the house afterwards.

People counteract the black streams in different ways – some people buy Raditechs – but I also put down six-millimetre crystal beads in the centre of the area of strongest influence, called the power-point. That seems to work.

'Bill Rich's problem was that he had lines all over the shop. All over his property. But there was one particularly bad area. There were two black streams crossing under his electricity metre in the hallway – toilet area. The crossing line, where these harmful rays cross, is much more dangerous than having just one single line. It was very, very powerful. I normally put down just a few crystals, but there I had to put down sixty-two crystals around a six-hundred metre circle. If I didn't get the exact centre, it's possible it didn't work completely. And, you know, with crystals this small, rabbits can move them. I'm not interested in the occult. I think it's a scientific thing with a scientific explanation.

'It's worth mentioning, with reference to the tiny crystals being easily moved, that all ancient standing stones have quartz in them. I've dowsed around these sites and there's certainly a benign feel to them. Who knows what these ancients were doing when they put up these whacking great stones, but it's certainly true there's no chance of any of them being accidentally moved.'

*

Dickie Dodds wasn't the only dowser to visit Heol Fanog. Since the Riches moved in, several were drawn to the property by the bizarre confluence of leys. Peter Davies was one who had been dowsing consistently around the country since the mid-seventies and while his findings paralleled those of Dickie Dodds, he added another perspective on the link between the leys and the phenomena manifesting within the house.

Davies first realized he had a talent for dowsing when he left the RAF just after the war. One day, for a bit of sport, he decided to go out with an old friend in Camarthen using twigs to look for water like the dowsers he had read about. His response was so powerful the twigs flew out of his hands. Even so, it took him almost thirty years to take it up seriously. He says he has no explanation for his skill as a dowser, which has been proved all over the country, he just accepts it.

*

The testimony of Peter Davies, dowser: 'The first thing I noticed when I got to Heol Fanog was all the energy lines. There was a heck of a lot of them all round there and most of it was harmful radiation – very, very bad. In fact, I'd go so far as to say it was the worst of all the places I have ever dowsed in around twenty years as a dowser. A lot of it is caused by underwater rivers in that area. Even if a river crosses a hundred miles underground you'll still feel the results on the surface. It's really to do with the magnetic fields changing. Quartz can do it too, and caverns can change it as well. It's just like a cathode ray tube when you put a charge at one end.

'I was intrigued by Heol Fanog's reputation as a haunted house. I've had experience of other houses with reputations for being haunted. They get cold, ghosts never leave the area. And they've all had trouble with energy lines. It seems to me that these spirits tend to feed off these negative rays, and a lot of lower earthbound entities as well. They seem to get stuck in the earth's radiation. They collect. It also seems to me that people tend to draw them, particularly if they're not very well. Any sort of sickness, physical and psychological, brings things in. That applies to anybody. I believe in this from my own experience.

'Sometimes the feeling from the harmful rays is so powerful I can feel it in m body without using a rod. I feel quite sick – chesty, coughing, that sort of thing. I call it using my body as a rod, but the best way to do it is with rods or a pendulum. Heol Fanog is a very nasty spot – I certainly wouldn't live there. When I walked up the pathway the first time I visited it, I felt violently sick. There was a fellow parking his car near the house and I ran back to him and told him not to leave it there, to go thirty yards up the road where it was safer. I have never known a pool of such harmful radiation. And I would never live there under any circumstances.'

*

Throughout all the time they were in Heol Fanog, Bill and Liz Rich compiled snippets of information, theories and advice. They felt if they could in some way get a handle of the cause of the phenomena they could find a way to rid themselves of it. Yet, strangely, as the information piled up, the picture grew murkier. Was it a scientific cause: underground radiation? Or a religious cause: spirits and demons? The answer seemed to elude them constantly.

Chapter 8

Between July 1991 and the spring of 1993, Heol Fanog seemed to be resting. The apparition of the old woman, the footsteps, smells and temperature changes were all long gone. The tall, black figure glimpsed by Liz made no reappearance, and the threat and sense of evil that presence carried with it had vanished. Yet Bill and Liz still felt all was not right with the house.

There was an uncomfortable atmosphere, which they couldn't seem to dispel however much they redecorated or cleaned. Bill could describe it only as a sense of anticipation, as if something was watching and waiting. Occasionally, Liz saw things out among the trees around the house. Shapes, dark figures. She would blink and they would be gone. And for most of the time, the Riches were plagued with the most terrible nightmares. One in particular was experienced by both of them and returned to haunt them several times.

They would be loading all their possessions into the car one last time as they prepared to set off for a bright, new place. Heol Fanog lowered darkly behind them as Bill and Liz finally piled the children into the back seat and then they sped away with a feeling of relief. For an interminable period, they hurtled around the lanes until, bizarrely, they found themselves outside the house once more. As they glanced up the long drive they saw themselves still there, trapped in the house, pressed against the windows, screaming…

Yet there was nothing tangible, certainly nothing compared to what they had been through before, and so they attempted to dismiss it and tried to kick-start their lives as best they could. Bill's work picked up slightly, although instead of selling to Paris and Los Angeles his work was now available at car boot sales and small shops across the southwest. The electricity drain, however, remained as disconcertingly high as ever.

It was at this time that Liz discovered she was pregnant again. As with her previous pregnancies, it wasn't planned, but despite the pressure they both knew a third child would bring they still welcomes it as something positive. Yet the prospect of a new birth didn't deflect their thoughts as much as they might have hoped.

Laurence, however, was progressing in leaps and bounds. He was his enjoying his job at a local hotel, and whenever Bill met him it seemed like the old times. There was no sign of the tormented child who had stayed at Heol Fanog, and that convinced Bill he had done the right thing in driving Laurence from the house. Even in the quiet times they were troubled by memories of what had gone before. When the atmosphere was particularly unsettling, they would phone David Holmwood for reassurance, but although it helped them cope, they couldn't shake the feeling that Heol Fanog would soon awaken again

*

Bill's testimony: 'I never felt that "horror thing" for almost two years, but I felt as if there was something there. Lots of things were happening, apart from the very evil influence that I could always feel but never saw. And Liz could see it – that tall, black figure – but she never felt it strongly. Things were happening, but always on the edges. Every time we had a problem in the house we would phone up David, or Anita, for prayer, and we would have a release. Yet it was a strange time. We were told so many things. David told us we're here to judge saints or angels. Anita told us we'd been through this to become exorcists ourselves. I mean, Anita told us so many things... She said what had happened in the house was because Satan wanted Liz to be a medium pulling up demons from hell, and I was supposed to be the director of this demonic crew for the Anti-Christ – sort of hell's air traffic controller. It was just too much.'

*

In spring 1993, when the evenings were still tinged with the bite of winter, the Riches had their fears confirmed. It was an evening shortly after 7:30, and the sky was dark and starless. As usual, the only sound that could be heard in Heol Fanog was the thrashing of the trees in the wind from the hills. Liz was upstairs with the children while Bill was in the kitchen, preparing a salad for the evening meal on the small work surface next to the sink.

Over the months Bill had learned to use mechanical tasks to free his mind from the constant worry and sense of threat. It was a Zen act of blank tranquillity, the slicing of a tomato, the washing of a lettuce; a quiet escape.

As he peeled a carrot, humming to himself, a movement on the periphery of his vision broke his calm thoughts. He recognized the signals instantly – when the apparitions came, it always happened the same way. A slight shift in the corner of his eye. A glance. An image of horror burnt into his retina. A blink. Gone, with just the memory to torment him forever. The worst thing was, he could never *not* look. It forced him to see, while his thoughts were screaming, Don't look! You'll only regret it!

With a sinking heart, as that familiar buzz of fear intruded on his peace, Bill felt his head creak round involuntarily in the direction of the movement. Only this time it was different. The apparition didn't disappear.

Emerging from the hallway was a breathtakingly beautiful woman. She was tall and slender with her hands pressed together in prayer. A long, white, diaphanous gown flowed over her body, barely hiding her form. Her lips were full, her eyes large and dark, her features ravishingly attractive.

The moment she appeared, Bill felt the mood of the room change; there was an aura of charged sexuality around her, flowing out to wrap itself around him. Bill felt instinctively that she wanted him; to follow her; to give himself up to her. Temptation.

He held back and watched. The figure didn't look at him, gave no sign he was there. She glided from the doorway to the hall, across the kitchen into the sitting room. The journey took around five seconds.

Bill snapped his attention back to the salad. *I'm not following.* And then: *She was so beautiful.* A heartbeat. *I'm not following. I'm not bothered!*

With calm, regular breathing, Bill controlled himself and then stepped out of the kitchen and walked up the stairs, without once glancing into the sitting room. In the nursery, he told Liz what he had seen.

'I didn't think it could be over,' she replied, staring blankly at a toy. Her comment was flat, almost mechanical, and somehow that made the moment worse.

A few minutes later, Liz wearily phoned David Holmwood to tell him what had happened. He seemed unsurprised. 'It was a Spirit of Seduction,' he said bluntly. It was trying to tempt Bill. Who knows what would have happened if he had followed? But he insisted they prayed together and that made Liz feel better for a while.

As Bill and Liz discussed the apparition, it added to the fears they had felt since the earliest days of the haunting – that whatever was in Heol Fanog was trying to split them up.

'We've got to be strong, Bill,' Liz said, grasping her husband's hand. 'We can't afford to let it break us up.'

Bill nodded in agreement. 'I know. If that happens, we're lost.'

They prayed together for deliverance and then entwined themselves together in bed until the first light broke through the curtains.

*

From the moment David Holmwood and Anita Dick had 'cleansed' Heol Fanog, the painting in the studio drew Bill incessantly, even when the demands on his time and energy in the rest of the house were growing stronger. His masterpiece had become an obsession that dominated his mind, and when he was in the studio in the day or during the long hours of the night, he painted with a frenzy that bypassed conscious thought. When he closed his eyes, he saw colours; wherever he was he could smell the pungent, greasy aroma of his oils.

As it neared completion, images began to appear out of the tangled design, a hand, a leg; gradually, a figure took shape on the right-hand side of the painting. It was a man, trapped so tightly in the snaking tendrils, which resembled arteries or veins, there was no hope of escape.

When the last stroke had been completed, Bill plopped his brush in to soak, wiped his hands on a rag and took a step back. The painting took his breath away – it *was* his masterpiece. Yet strangely he felt no jubilation, just a weary acceptance that the work was finally over. It was deflating, and he wondered if it had something to do with the painting's melancholy atmosphere. Strangely, as his eyes wandered over it, it was almost like he was seeing it for the first time. With his other work he had been conscious of it taking shape, but this one had developed in a fog; he remembered the first brushstroke, and the final one, and that was all. He wallowed in the detail, the heart, the tears, that trapped, miserable figure, and then he had a sudden disturbing thought.

Is that me? Is that how I feel about my life in this place?

Trapped. Suffering. Anguish. Bill sat in his old armchair and closed his eyes.

*

As the spring of 1993 eased into the hot summer, which leached the colour from the fields and hills around the house, their nightmares gradually became more lucid and powerful, and more disturbing. Bill's seemed so real it was as if he had been transported somewhere else. After waking they stayed with him, instead of fading like normal dreams.

The central image was a beaked or hook-nosed figure, half-man, half-bird, like the Egyptian Falcon-god Horus. The figure was immobile, like a statue, but Bill always had a sensation of a presence; he was sure it was alive. In the same way, he was convinced it was threatening, although he didn't see any proof of that.

It came back to him night after night, and after a few days it became apparent that it wasn't going to go away.

Things changed one July afternoon as Bill stood in the gloom of the kitchen. The house was chilly despite the heat of the summer, but through the open window he could see the yellow grass, which had swept across the once neatly tended garden, and on the breeze came the fresh scent of the countryside. Bill closed his eyes and inhaled.

The image of the thing with the head of a bird appeared suddenly in his mind. It was such a powerful sensation Bill's eyes flashed open in shock. It was as if a trigger had been pulled. There was a vertiginous feeling of something rushing in that made him feel giddy and then he felt bands of tension tightening across his chest. It was his body responding to something he felt on a subconscious level – the sudden change in the atmosphere of the house. No longer simply uncomfortable, it had become charged and dark once more. The hairs on his arm tingled erect. Bill felt like he was suffocating.

Terrified, he turned to rush from the kitchen and in that instant he saw it there with him. It was watching him, still like a statue, but on some level he didn't understand. He could sense both mockery and threat. Bill felt it was telling him that it had returned. That it could not be beaten.

His head whirling, Bill scrambled upstairs to find Liz. She was in the playroom with the children. The happiness drained from her face when she saw Bill's expression.

'Pray with me,' he said.

'What?'

'Pray with me!'

Bill took her by the hand and led her into the next bedroom. While the children played happily together, they closed their eyes and prayed for strength as David Holmwood had showed them. A second later, the thing was there, and this time they both saw it.

Liz’s hands fell away in horror. ‘That’s it Bill! That’s the thing –‘

‘Keep praying!’

There was a trembling desperation in his voice as he willed the thing to go away. Next door, the children laughed wildly. A toy crashed to the floor.

‘It’s not going, Bill.’

He could hear fear and despair in her words for the first time in nearly two years. Bill glanced sideways, there were tears streaming down Liz’s cheeks. That fired his resolve, but when his eyes fell once more on the shape his bravery bled away.

‘Please go,’ he begged. ‘In the name of Jesus –‘

And then it was gone, winking out like a candle being snuffed. But the atmosphere it had brought with it remained.

*

Whatever it was, or whatever it truly represented, to Bill it was a sign that the ‘horror’ was back. Once more they were thrust into that whirlpool of anxiety, but their gut instinct told them the worst was yet to come. The bird-headed thing, which Liz realized was the same as the dark, evil figure she had seen, left an atmosphere like treacle and a feeling of threat stronger than anything they had felt before.

Desperate to rid himself of the latest manifestation, Bill called David Holmwood, and they prayed together on the phone. As they talked, the figure appeared once again, like it was responding to Bill’s words. Its arms were by its side, it was rigid and staring; Bill couldn’t understand why it never moved. He described it to Mr Holmwood and then felt a sudden chill when the chaplain replied, ‘It’s here, Bill. I can see it too.’

Bill tried to hold himself calm, but the feeling radiating off the figure was so menacing it made him shake. He felt it was trying to drag him away from the phone.

Their prayers grew more intense. Suddenly Bill saw something start to happen: droplets of liquid splashed on its head and shoulders and began to stream down its torso.

'It has water on it,' Bill said curiously.

'No,' Holmwood's voice sounded distant. 'I have just put the blood of Christ on it.'

The figure started to shrink as the droplets fell on it, but when they stopped praying it grew again, and this time its arms were folding in defiance.

The phone line crackled. 'If you do not obey, you will be destroyed!' Holmwood barked.

The thing continued to grow; Bill felt the threat in the room grow with it until his breath started to catch in his throat.

Bill was concentrating on the figure so intently he missed what David Holmwood was saying until the last '... condemned by the death of Christ. I will put a wall of fire around you.'

Flames suddenly erupted from the floor. Bill felt no heat from them, but he was so startled he almost dropped the phone. The blaze engulfed the figure and when the flames finally flickered into nothing, a few seconds later, the figure was gone.

'It's gone,' Bill croaked. He realized he was trembling like he had a physical shock. The psychic atmosphere of threat disappeared a few seconds later like a bad smell dispersing in the breeze.

*

David Holmwood's testimony: 'I did sense a presence in Heol Fanog when I first visited and once I even saw it out of the corner of my eye. It was a seven-foot tall dark, angelic presence. Not a good angel. It was very dark with a hooked nose. No angel's wings. It was a tall figure and certainly not human. I sensed that in the kitchen area, and I know Bill said he heard footsteps around there. It quite often happens that you can see things in the corner of your eye because that is a very sensitive area. If you look straight on, there's nothing there. But if you look back and to one side, you can see it again.

'Having expelled this being in the name of Jesus, it kept coming back. It must have been a senior being – it wasn't going to be pushed around. I don't think it was Satan, but it must have been one of the senior entities. Bill phoned me up and said there was a presence there. He described the being I had seen, which looked a little Egyptian, bizarrely. Gradually it became more distinct in the way he could describe it. We prayed over the phone. In His name, I told him to go.

'Bill said, "He's laughing at you. He just won't go." I asked the Lord to put a wall of flame around that place, to cover the house with the blood of Jesus and to put guardian angels around that place. Bill could see the drops of blood falling on him. Then I accused this creature, on behalf of his master, of being guilty of causing the death of Jesus. Bill said, "He's shaking." I then asked the Lord to put a wall of fire around the angelic being, and as I did that Bill said, "He's going up in smoke." I said, "If you don't go, you will be destroyed." He went and that was the final item.'

*

They only saw the beaked figure once more, many months later, standing on a hillside watching the house. Yet at that moment, Bill felt they had won a crucial victory against the evil threatening the house. Defeat, he was sure, would have meant the end of all of them.

Bill's sense of relief seemed to be echoed by a change in the mood of the house; the dark atmosphere didn't disappear completely, but it receded enough to allow in some light, which made them both feel something profound had happened.

*

Bill's testimony: 'This beaked figure, I could see it so clearly. It looked rather like Horus, the Egyptian god – that's the only way I can describe it. It was stationary, like a statue, but I distinctly remember the drips suddenly appearing on it…'

*

By that time, the Riches were very sensitive to the mood of Heol Fanog. Although it seemed better, they knew from the background buzz that the fear would soon be back. David Holmwood had been a part of their lives for nearly two years, but the latest manifestation made them realize their situation was just as desperate as it had been when he arrived.

'David's a lovely man, but he's not doing anything to rid us of the problem,' Bill said, as he and Liz sat in the kitchen discussing the way forward. 'I'm thankful for the support he's given us, but we've got to find a way to stop it for good.'

Liz agreed. 'Look, he's had enough time, but we've got to let go.'

'Who do we look to next?' Bill asked desperately. 'Do we just keep trying indefinitely? I wish we could get away from this place.'

'We have to, until we find something that works, somebody who can make sense of it all and drive it all away. Giving up isn't an option. Giving up means we lose everything… and I mean *everything*. We have to keep fighting however weary we get.'

The fire in Liz's voice gave Bill hope. He knew in his heart that their strength came in the two of them standing shoulder to shoulder. Whatever was in the house seemed determined to split them up – the stresses, the increasing problems in all aspects of their lives, the Spirit of Seduction the most tangible form, all heaped on top of each other until it would have crushed weaker couples. Together they could keep fighting. Perhaps they could even win.

*

Bill's testimony: 'During the two years after David and Anita first exorcized the house, the electricity was wild – that was something we couldn't understand. They said it was like if you had a house on fire – it takes a long time for the smell of smoke to go. Those things were being said. They really didn't want to admit they had failed. And I think if we hadn't gone to someone else – which we didn't want to because David was such a wonderful, loving man – it would have gone on forever and ever. David, like the others, appeared to stop the situation for a period of time, but then it would come back. We needed someone who could finally complete the job.'

*

The pressure was growing on Bill from several directions but he felt it deepest in his painting. After he had finished what he still referred to as his 'masterpiece' he felt empty but hopeful that he could carry on and create other great works of art. It soon became apparent that that was not to be the case. The constantly draining money worries, the repeated small blows of having young children around the house, the compacted layers of dread, all helped to sap his energy. But he felt, in his darker moments, that there was more to it. It was like the house itself was stopping him working; it had allowed him to finish his masterpiece, for whatever reason, but that was the end of it. Like the mysterious infirmity to his fingers that had recurred many times, it seemed like the house was out to prevent him creating, as if all his art represented was not in tune with the house's mood.

He felt his energy draining in the same way the power was being sucked out of the house. When they first moved in he would chop wood in the garden for an hour and prepare a waist-high pile of logs. Now, when he went out, he would complete two logs and be so exhausted he would have to lie down. It went beyond listlessness, or lethargy; it was a sapping of his spirit.

He couldn't fight it any more, but he felt he also had to make a sacrifice for the sake of Liz and his family. He decided to give up the thing that had been vitally important to him for most of his life. In a fit of despair and anger he realized he had to burn the desire to paint out of him. He retrieved his brushes from where he had thrown them, stormed into his studio and selected one of his old paintings. There was no use for it any more – that part of his life was going.

He hung the painting in the centre of the room and then began to paint over it. He had no idea what he was creating. He let that deep, creative power come through him. His brush flashed wildly; he used his hands, grabbing palmfuls of oil and smearing it across the canvas. He was like a madman lost in a world of reds and blues and blacks.

After twenty minutes of frenzied activity, he lurched backwards and collapsed into his chair. It was finished. He looked up at the canvas, and the image filled his entire vision.

A blazing white cross glared out majestically from a turbulent background of browns, blacks, purples and greens, all merging into a whirlpool which represented the emotions that terrible house generated. But the cross was the dominant image. Staring at it, he felt a flare of hope in the dark night of his despair. The title for the piece came instantly. *Testimony.*

*

Bill's testimony: 'It was terrible trying to come to terms with the fact that my painting wasn't going to go much further. On that night, and during the next day, I realized that I had to make a decision that I could either have Liz or I could continue with my artistic ambitions. Either I stayed in the house with Liz and the children during a hard time, or I had to make a decision to get out because I simply wanted to paint. And that same evening I threw my brushes out of the window. Some of them are still out there somewhere.

'I knew right then that I was going to go back into jail in one way or another – I've never been in jail, but in jail in the sense that my mind was going to be stuck for thought and inspiration for some considerable time. It was very, very hard to give up the art. It was terribly hard because I had been building up to it all my life. But there are much more important things and I'm so glad it's happened like that because that's the only thing that's kept Liz and I together. Since then there had been no conflict of "I want" or anything like that. She's been thinking of me and I've been thinking of her – and that's the only way to get through, really. With love.'

*

Meanwhile, Heol Fanog's electrical problems were continuing in force. Bill had found himself immersed in a full-scale battle with Swalec. The company admitted the meter readings were way above average – to the point of it being a business bill – yet it still insisted Bill was using the power in some way. Swalec was responsible for any problems with the feed into the house, but Bill had to accept responsibility for his appliances, and as the company had repeatedly checked its supply lines and equipment and found no problem, then the fault *must* – they said – lie within Heol Fanog.

For his part, Bill hired an expert to check every appliance in the house. None of them was at fault, and even when everything was switched off, the meter was still whizzing round. Something was sucking up the power to tremendous levels.

The meter was changed to a token-feed, but it was apparent that wasn't the source of the problem. Bill was ramming tokens into it constantly, and even when he left it empty the power continued to drain away. When he next came to put tokens in, he found a massive debit that had to be cleared before he could power the house.

After he had exhausted all rational explanations for the power drain, Bill said to Liz, 'I think whatever is in here is *feeding* on the power. Does that sound crazy?'

'After what has happened, Bill, I would believe anything,' Liz replied exhaustedly. 'Why not this? There's got to be some explanation.'

Bill shuffled the pile of bills and correspondence with Swalec around the kitchen table, trying to unlock some kind of sense from all the reports and facts and figures. 'We've got to do something about it. It's breaking us, financially. We can't carry on paying £750 a quarter.'

'Look, we'll get through it. My parents have started to help. They're going to contribute to the bills until we get our heads above water. Don't keep whatever's here. I mentioned the problem with the electricity when I called Bridget Buscombe.'

'Oh?'

'She never had any problem at all. Just regular bills. It started when we moved in.'

Bill tried to weigh up the implications of Liz's words. 'So what are we going to do?' he thought aloud.

Swalec refused to back down. Bill refused to pay because there was no way he could be using the power. In the end he found a solicitor in nearby Crickhowell, Glyn Maddocks, who would fight his case on legal aid, but he warned Bill the company would never admit to be a supernatural cause. That would open them up to thousands of bogus claims from people trying to cut their bills. And could any of it be proved?

'We have to fight whatever happens,' Bill said. 'We owe them hundreds of pounds already. I can't afford to pay.'

Mr Maddocks, however, was intrigued by the case, and when Bill left the office he felt they finally had someone on their side.

*

The testimony of Glyn Maddocks, solicitor, of Gabb & Co, Crickhowell: 'Mr Rich had been an existing client and when he decided to become legalistic in this matter he approached me. I am sceptical about the supernatural and it seems to me there must be some sort of scientific explanation. What Mr Rich did – which is not very exact, but good enough to make a point – was tot up the amount of devices in the house and how much electricity each one should use. And even with all of them going all the time seven days a week they would not have used enough electricity to explain what the meter was showing. On that basis it was obvious something was going wrong.

'The problem is Swalec is taking a very negative attitude to this sort of thing. The company just sends out bills and expects people to pay. I would have expected that Swalec would have been far more sympathetic. It seems obvious that someone with a couple of light bulbs and a TV can't consume this amount of electricity each week.

‘It could be that the problem is not unique. Perhaps Bill Rich is the only one creating waves. The average bill is £27 a month in Wales. Mine is about £100 and I put it down to the kids, but you couldn’t get Swalec to come along and help you if it’s not the average. The company has indicated it is not prepared to cut Bill off, which is something. But Swalec hasn’t been able to help identify what the problem is. You would think a monopoly would have the technology to check where something like this is going wrong. It is total arrogance, a very unhelpful attitude. Perhaps it is simply the fact the company does not want to set a precedent and get deluged with similar queries. Who knows? Bill is paying £7 a week at the moment, and we are waiting for further tests on the meter, but after that we are back to square one.’

*

The testimony of South Wales Electricity, as delivered by the company spokesman, Haydn Price: ‘Numerous tests were carried out by the company at Heol Fanog. We checked all supplies in the house. The meter is working perfectly. From the meter into the house is Mr Rich’s responsibility, but we are sure the meter is reading accurately. We are quite satisfied there is no leakage of any sort. We have never experienced anything like this before. Energy advisers were sent in and we’ve carried out many, many tests. We have done everything we are obliged to do and therefore the obligation is with Mr Rich for what the meter says. But we also want to be quite fair and sort out a reasonable way for him to pay.’

*

By the end of the summer of 1993, things seemed more hopeless than they had ever been. Nothing had changed after nearly four years of spiritual, emotional and psychological struggle. The evil was still there, refusing to be driven from the house, threatening everything they held dear. And they were still alone in their battle, facing up to the dark with no idea of who could help them or what they could do next. In desperation, Liz found a number for an organization called the Christian World Revival, a theological society that sent missionaries all over the globe. Her plea for an exorcist was accepted without surprise and she was given the number of one of the country's experts in the field, Dr John Aston. At her lowest ebb, she dialled.

Chapter 9

Liz spoke to John Aston on the phone for close to an hour. He wanted to know everything they had been through at Heol Fanog. At the end of the conversation, he asked Liz to leave it with him and he would decide what to do after prayer. Liz felt a little deflated that his response wasn't immediate, but she felt hopeful he would take up their cause.

In the end it took him three months of prayer and planning before he could agree a date to visit Heol Fanog. During that time Bill and Liz grew increasingly despairing. They felt isolated once more and the atmosphere and attacks were growing more intense. It was hard for them to explain their situation to outsiders because there were few tangible signs, yet they felt the assaults as if they had been physically beaten. There would be days of electric tension hanging in the air and then suddenly it would break like a storm. The children would become disturbed, crying, unable to sleep, unable even to settle. Bill and Liz would feel their emotions raging across a wide if bleak spectrum, from irritation and anger through to despair. Bill felt like he had been grabbed by the shoulders and spun round so hard he made grooves in the stone flags; the disorientation verged on the brink of madness. And through it all the watcher continued to watch, sometime distant, sometimes so close they felt if they turned round suddenly they would catch him behind them. During those times they could almost taste the hatred pouring out of that presence, and its potency made them fear for their lives. After the attack was over, there was no peace, just a return to that electric tension before the next one. It left them exhausted and with little chance of recovering.

When John Aston finally called to arrange his exorcism, the Riches felt their saviour had suddenly ridden onto the battlefield. They invested all their hope in him like they had with so many of the other visitors to Heol Fanog.

*

The testimony of John Aston, Baptist Minister: 'Bill and Liz's case was referred to me by Sue Lees of the Christian World Revival, with some information. More was added by Bill and Liz. I mentioned to Sue that from time to time I had to make decisions about taking things on. Afterwards, Sue told me that while a colleague, Tony, was praying for me, she saw a child pulling, not my hand, but the sleeve of my pullover round my hand, so that I could not use my hand. In my right hand I had the sword of the Spirit which could cut through the irritation of my left hand being constrained. That was a relatively small matter, a minor spirit, a distraction, and could be overcome with patience. Sue had supposed that this picture was guidance or warning and what to expect when I went to Heol Fanog, not guidance to keep out.

'Her picture was preceded by pictures of knots in an intricate pattern, first Celtic knots and then Egyptian knots, which were actually the swathing around a dead body, a mummy.

'When Sue prayed with her husband about the matter, he had the idea of a den of formidable lions. I wrote at the time: "I am going into it – I do not have much choice, but with God it will be OK." The picture reminded her husband of the Beast in Revelations 13.1-10 which had the mouth of a lion. I had read the passage that morning, while reading through Revelation.'

*

Liz and Bill always loved to have animals around, but so many of their pets had died or gone crazy that they were wary of bringing any more into the house. Even so, Liz decided at that point she wanted a dog. She felt it would be a positive influence amongst all the malice that filled Heol Fanog, and it was also a practical protection against intruders in such an isolated spot. They chose a Doberman, which they christened Beau, and at first his wilderness and antics seemed just what they needed.

Not long after Beau had settled in, the Riches noticed he was acting strangely around the kitchen and hallway, growling at things that no one else could see, the fur on his back bristling. Over the days his condition worsened, until they were regularly disturbed by his howls and anxious pacing in circles, as if he was trapped in a cage. Finally, he couldn't move from his place in front of the boiler, where he lay constantly shaking. The Riches noticed he deteriorated as the day of John Aston's exorcism approached.

*

On the 29 July 1993, Bill met John Aston in the Brecon to show him the meandering way up to the house. He was tall, slim and distinguished-looking, in his seventies, with an aquiline nose and a studious, tranquil nature. He came with three assistants: his wife, also in her seventies, and a younger man and his wife from his church.

Liz had taken the children out of the house for a picnic with her mother, as she had during all the previous exorcisms. Bill and Liz were adamant Ben and Rebecca would be shielded from all the strangeness and the terror of Heol Fanog, and according to the testimonies of teachers and health visitors, they succeeded.

When the party from Brecon arrived back at Heol Fanog, Bill felt as if their house had been waiting for them; there was a powerful sense of anticipation. He recognized it from every other time someone had come to Heol Fanog to help.

The ritual was also familiar. John Aston and his assistants first got the feel of the place around the grounds before exploring inside. When they reached the playroom – what used to be Ben's bedroom, where Liz had repeatedly seen the spectre of the old woman they believed to be Mrs Holbourn – Mrs Aston suddenly went rigid. 'I have a feeling someone died in this room,' she said.

No one else spoke. Bill stayed in the background, feeling the tension acutely, as if someone were sticking pins in his flesh. The house was still, and although the garden was washed in sunlight it was devoid of any birdsong.

The party processed to the studio. Bill could tell they were all growing increasingly anxious; their faces were taught and pale, their arms tight by their sides. As soon as they reached the centre of the studio, Mrs Aston let out a sigh and shuddered. 'There is a strong evil presence in this room,' she said. The others nodded darkly.

John Aston suggested they sing an old Baptist hymn. Their voices sounded strange and lonely as they echoed around the dusty, sparse room. 'In the name of Jesus.... By the blood of Jesus... demons will have to flee... Hallelujah!'

Bill felt the mood shift slightly, as if whatever was there had moved to the corners of the room. He wondered if it was a defensive recoil or preparation for an attack. He pressed his nails into his palms to focus his mind. All he could think about was how he spent so much time alone in there, losing himself to the creative spirit. Had it always been there with him?

The atmosphere around the group was growing darker as they became more attuned to Heol Fanog. Venturing outside the house once more, they forced themselves to approach the ruins of the old manor house, which had so terrified other visitors. Bill could tell from their apprehension that they sensed something. They stood among the ivy-clad stones where the sense of decay was palpable, and listened; the eerie stillness was unnerving. No birds sang. There, in the heart of the country, they could hear no sheep, no insects. But all of them agreed they were not alone.

'There's something quite unpleasant here.'

'A presence.'

'I can't identify it, but it is not good.'

Their voices droned on while Bill looked around him nervously.

They decided to sing another hymn, both to raise their own spirits and to proclaim the power that was on their side to anything which might have been there.

When they returned to the house in a subdued and introspective mood, Liz was waiting for them. She had sent the children off with her mother so she could be there when the exorcism was carried out. She was part of it; she felt wrong leaving all the responsibility to

Bill. She held hands with Bill briefly, a touch of support and strength before they moved anxiously to the house. It was almost time.

Bill and Liz were both asked if they believed Jesus Christ was their Lord and Saviour and, when they both affirmed, John Aston and his wife took Bill into the living room while Liz stayed with the other couple in the kitchen. Bill's heart was pounding madly. He wanted Liz there at his side so he could hold her hand, face up to what was to come together. Apart from her, he felt lost, weak. Their strength was in unity.

John Aston started to talk in a soft, soothing voice, but Bill wasn't aware of his words. His attention was lost to what was happening to Liz in the kitchen. He could hear things that unnerved him, then terrified him. Every fibre of his being was telling him to rush in to help her, but every time his leg muscles flexed or he leaned forward, John Aston placed a gentle, but restraining hand on his arm and whispered, 'Leave them to it.'

In the kitchen, the couple had sat Liz in a chair by the window. Although neither of the Riches realized it, the visitors felt it obvious that Liz was playing a fundamental role in what was happening in Heol Fanog.

She sat with her head back and her eyes closed, but although the couple tried to get her to relax she remained rigid with tension. The assistants spoke to her constantly in the same soft voice John Aston used, and they seemed to be interested in something she had mentioned, in passing, to John Aston on the telephone.

'My eyes? Why do you want to know about my eyes?' Bill could hear the growing fear in her voice. The couple tried to calm her once more and then pressed her to continue. 'Yes… it's true,' Liz replied tentatively. 'I've always felt I had some power in my eyes, or some power within me that I channelled through my eyes. When I was younger I always felt I could get people to do what I wanted if I looked at them in a certain way. When I was working as a herbalist, I found I could heal people with my eyes, or it seemed that way. I believed it.'

There was a long silence and then the couple mumbled something to each other and reached some kind of agreement. The man turned back to Liz. 'The spirit of the eyes is in you,' he said.

'What do you mean?'

The man ignored her question. 'Do you believe that Jesus Christ is your Lord and Saviour?' he asked again.

In that moment Bill's body filled with ice. The voice that echoed back into the living room in reply was not his wife's. It didn't even sound wholly human.

'*No. Nothing to do with me.*'

The masculine voice was like a rasp n metal, crackling and incredibly old, filled with equal measures of hatred and mockery. It was followed by laughter, horrible, inhuman.

Bill threw John Aston off and ran into the kitchen. The couple were standing back, watching Liz's face, which was twisted with malice.

'Oh my God!' Bill cried.

The terrible laughter echoed from her mouth once more.

*

Bill's testimony: 'There was a voice which was not her voice. And it answered the question about Jesus Christ, then laughed, horrible laughter. That sounds too hard to believe, because it is what you would expect if you were watching some stupid, creepy movie. But it was that voice, and it wasn't Liz's voice, and I was very, very worried about her. I wanted to go in and help her in some way, but I couldn't. This passed off, and the voice stopped and Liz was crying. And the two people were standing beside her with their hands on her. I can't remember a thing that happened after that moment.

'Later, John Aston and his wide came into the kitchen to have Communion. They had brought a can of red wine and I felt like drinking a barrel of it. We broke the bread and had the wine and thanked Jesus who had the power to make this place bright. And then we went into prayer. They put their hands on the back of my head and I quite physically felt the power coming from them. It made me realize the power that good has too. This went on for some time as they worked their way around the house. They asked me to say a prayer and, shortly after, they left.'

*

Liz's testimony: 'I don't remember any of what happened to me in the kitchen. All I can recall now is going into the living room and doing the Eucharist with John Aston. I had my eyes closed and I was crying my eyes out down there because I could see this old lady in black – the one I had seen before in the playroom – and she was floating above us. I had my eyes closed, but I could see this. I was crying and crying because I wanted so much for her to be set free. It was like she pleading for help and I think she was set free at that point because I wasn't aware of her anymore. Weird. It was all a weird, frightening experience. I'm glad I can't remember what happened to me.'

*

Afterwards, the mood of the house seemed to brighten once again; this time, though, Liz and Bill were more optimistic, although they still felt everything was not quite right. They had never been through such a harrowing experience before, and the extent of their psychological torment made them feel that finally they had done enough to rid themselves of the horror. They phoned John Aston the next day to thank him for what he had done, explaining that the threat had gone; despite the occasional gloomy period, the house was brighter and the air almost seemed to sing.

*

Extract from the diary of Dr John Aston:

*

27 July 1993: Wife phoned to say that her husband is very fearful. She feels stressed. The dog is 'crazy', jumping around, and she notices that a lot of hair is falling out from the goat – a sign on emotional stress in goats. The atmosphere has changed dramatically in the last three or four days. They have experienced strange things in the house for the last four years, but nothing like this – it is quite different this time. Apprehension. Both of them have always regarded themselves as sensitive to surroundings… Often, they have a sense that the house has a life of its own and that they are intruding into it.

As we prayed with Bill and Liz – feeling of grief, perhaps of occupants of the house? Of graves? A broken heart? Impression of a carving of an acorn with a split in it. 'Do not let your hearts be troubled, neither let them be afraid.' Impression of a natural fountain coming up out of the ground. Zech 13.1-2 'a fountain will be opened to purify the descendants of David from their sin and idolatry…'

*

29 July 1993: Visit to the house. As Bill and Liz were praying yesterday, they saw a light above the ruins of the manor house, but not reaching it…

While J and I were talking to the husband, B and J were talking to the wife. After they had taken her through repentance, several demons manifested and were easily dealt with.

We celebrated Communion together. I invited them to acknowledge their ancestor's sins (including his grandfather's abortions), which they did in an ill-defined way. Also repented of bringing the mediums to the house. I prayed for those who had lived in the house. I prayed over water and salt, mixed them, and we went through the house, praying in each room and sprinkling. In a few places B or J had a 'feeling' that there was something about it, but of 'energy' (psychic?) rather than of actual evil. One corresponded to the place where the mediums said the ley lines crossed. Then to the remains of the manor farm, and round their 'patch', praying and sprinkling water. The dog was tied up, very frisky and trying to get to us, but probably only playful. Neither it nor the goats showed any reaction to the brine.

Prayed for each of them and anointed. They were aware of warmth and other feelings.

*

The day after John Aston's exorcism, Bill called the local dog warden, Liz Jones, to see if she could call to check for some physical cause for Beau's strange actions over the last few weeks. When Liz Jones arrived she chatted to Liz Rich about the dog for a while, until Liz Rich suddenly asked, 'How does the house feel today?'

'It's funny, I was just admiring it,' Liz Jones said. 'The air's clear and fresh like there's been a heavy storm. It's really pleasant.'

'There *was* a storm here at the weekend,' Liz said. 'There was an exorcism.' She expected a dumbfounded reaction, but the dog warden didn't seem taken aback at all.

'You've had some problems as well, have you?' the dog warden said.

'What do you mean, "as well"?' Liz asked curiously.

'Oh, I know Heol Fanog well,' Liz Jones replied.

*

The testimony of Liz Jones, council dog warden, Brecon: 'Bridget Buscombe, who used to live in Heol Fanog before the Riches, was a very good friend of mine. In the summer of 1986 Bridget went away to work in Oxford for a while, and I would go up to the house every day to feed and water her animals. There were some sheep and a Shetland pony, so I had to keep going back and forth into the house to fetch buckets of water. I used to check around the house to make sure everything was OK, and water the plants, and things like that.

'I never used to like crossing the hallway and I never liked upstairs at all. But I always used to put it down to the normal feelings you would get in an empty house a long way from anywhere.

'The first time I was there on my own, I was in the kitchen and I heard what sounded like footsteps running along the landing upstairs. I just freaked. Then I thought for a moment and convinced myself it was knocking in the water pipes upstairs. Just to convince myself I went to the taps and turned them on. Then I made myself go upstairs. There was nothing there, nothing amiss. But when I was on the landing I always had this feeling that somebody was going past the foot of the stairs. I never felt bad in the lounge and not too bad in the kitchen. There was a strange feeling to different parts of the property, an eerie feeling. It was fine at the front of the house, but not at the back or near the ruins. I hated it if I had to go hunting for the animals.

'Well, this sound upstairs carried on whenever I went back. Although I kept telling myself it was just the pipes, in the end I was dreading going up there. I'd start to park the car at the end of the drive and walk up to the house because I thought I could get away quicker if I left it outside the gate. I never really considered why I thought that. I just wanted to do what I had to do and get out and go.

'Just before Christmas, when the frost came, I turned the water off just to be safe, so the pipes didn't freeze up. The next day when I went in, I heard the footsteps upstairs again – even though there was no water in the system, so it couldn't be the pipes banging. I freaked, completely, and just got out of there.

'My stepson Arwyn spent a lot of time at Heol Fanog as a child, and he always described it as an island of silence – there were times when the birds never sang. My husband lived there when her first came to Brecon and he didn't like it particularly either, although nothing happened to frighten him.

'It was funny because Bridget didn't tell me about the spinning-wheel – she didn't want to freak me when I was up there on my own – and I didn't tell her about the footsteps because I didn't want to freak her. We never discussed it until after she left, and then I told her what I felt about the place.

'The first time I met Bill and Liz Rich was very significant. The place certainly had a different feel to when Bridget and her son were there. It didn't have that threatening aura. When it was empty, it was almost as if it didn't want someone breaking its silence. It seemed quite happy being empty.

'But when I got the call that someone wanted help with a dog, and I saw the name Heol Fanog, my heart sank. I thought I'd said goodbye to that place. I kept finding things to do so I didn't have to go up there, but eventually I forced myself to go up on a Monday. I did my usual thing and parked outside the gate, but although the weather was quite normal, there was a different feel about the place, like there had just been a storm.'

*

The Riches decided they could use Heol Fanog's massive electricity drain as a faithful yardstick to measure the effectiveness of whoever tried to help, and after Dr Aston's visit there was still no change. Over the following few days, other signs manifested as the mood of the house grew more intense, and then, almost like a light flicking off, they felt the presence re-enter the house.

Liz Jones couldn't find anything wrong with Beau, so Bill took him to the local vet, who gave a similar diagnosis. Yet the dog was still barking, whimpering and shivering whenever he was in the house, driving up the tension so Bill and Liz could never ignore it and what it represented. Beau was acting exactly how they would act if they didn't have an intellect to control their responses. It seemed obvious that he was being attacked by whatever was in Heol Fanog, and that made them realize that John Aston's exorcism hadn't worked.

The day after the visit to the vet, they sat with Beau in the kitchen, trying to calm him after an extended bout of whimpering.

'Poor dog.' Liz stroked Beau's head and back; his skin rippled like water at her touch. She couldn't bear to see her pet suffering. 'It's our fault, isn't it?' she continued tearfully. 'We shouldn't have brought him in here. We knew what the house was like. We'd seen what had happened to the other animals. Why were we so stupid?'

'Because we're eternal optimists, that's why. Through all the crises, we just carry on doing normal things and trying to lead a normal life ready for when the light finally appears at the end of the tunnel. Beau's part of that. He's not just a pet. He's a symbol of what we're fighting for.'

'But he's suffering, Bill.'

At that moment, Beau suddenly stopped whimpering and sat bolt upright. The fur on his back bristled erect and his lips curled back from his teeth as a low, threatening grown rumbled deep in his throat. His eyes were fixed on something behind them. Instinctively, Bill and Liz whirled round together.

Beau was staring through the kitchen door to the darkened hallway near the foot of the stairs. There was nothing there.

'What has he seen?' Liz's voice was a sandpaper whisper.

They both stared intently into the empty space while Beau growled between them, terrified that something was going to appear.

'Can you feel it?' Bill said fearfully.

They could have been responding to Beau's defensive growling, but they both sensed a change in the room's mood. It appeared to be growing gloomier, as if folds of darkness were being wrapped around it, and the level of tension rose several notches. They stared into the hall, and stared and stared as the beating of their hearts filled their heads, waiting for something to happen. They both felt that if they could look into that space in the right way, maybe with a sudden sideways glance, they would see it waiting there for them. The evil thing.

The tableau was frozen like that for several seconds, and then suddenly the atmosphere seemed to crack and fall apart. Whatever had been there was retreating until another time, taking the darkness with it. Beau's growling caught in his throat and gradually he subsided like a deflating balloon to resume his pathetic whimpering.

'Lord help us,' Bill muttered.

*

When Liz headed out to look after the children, Bill couldn't bear to leave Beau on his own. He slid up next to Beau's mat in front of the boiler as the dog continued to shiver and cry. They stayed there together for five full minutes while Bill ruminated over his guilt at the dog's suffering until an idea began to develop in his head.

He leaned forward to place one hand on Beau's head and then said quietly, 'Jesus, whatever is bothering this dog, take the fear.'

The moment he removed his hand, Beau closed his eyes, lay down and went to sleep, almost like he had succumbed to his exhaustion. In disbelief, Bill watched the steady rise and fall of his back, the tranquillity of a rest without twitches or grumbles, which the dog had not experienced for days. Even then, Bill found it difficult to grasp that his prayer had worked. That something *he* had done in that nightmarish house had worked.

Then an almost triumphant sense of jubilation bubbled up through the ever-present dread and he was scrambling through the house to find Liz. When he located her with Ben and Rebecca he could barely find the words. 'Liz,' he said breathlessly, 'something remarkable has happened.'

*

Extracts from the diary of Dr John Aston:

*

4 August 1993: I phoned them, wife answered: 'The house still gets its moods. Things are not quite right. It still needs lots of prayer. During Communion I saw Mrs Holborn and a small boy, both looking very sad. They seemed to be suspended and looking down on us. Also, there was a black area on the left. I don't know what happened to them because I had to leave to look after the children.'

*

8 August 1993: Wife phone in distress: 'It's been awful and we can't stand much more. The dog has been wild and the children have been wound up. They are still not asleep and normally they would have been an hour or more ago. Can you find anyone who can help us?' (I had mentioned that possibility in the previous phone conversation.) She made no mention of any 'peculiar happenings' but many regard their condition as a result of the 'atmosphere'. For me, getting things right is largely, if not entirely, up to them. There seems to be no one in DH's church in whom they have confidence, yet it is regular support and guidance from a mature Christian that they need.

*

10 August 1993: Wife phoned to say that the situation is seriously affecting her husband – not so much herself. He is stuck with the idea that he is under a curse. Whatever he does, he is being hurt e.g., when he is looking for ways of earning money. Looking back over his life, he sees that doors have closed unaccountably.

I talked about possible sources of curses (mentioning a man who had been in Africa). She said that her husband had lived among the Australian Aborigines and had 'sort of married an Abo girl.' He has a tattoo on his leg from this time.

His father was one of the Dam Buster pilots and this is still on his mind – he reads anything he can find about it – perhaps he has a sense of guilt? (This confirms my judgement that now the primary need is for thorough counselling/ disciplining of the husband.)

*

In desperation, Bill placed another story about the electricity drain in the *Brecon and Radnor Express* to stimulate enquiries from people who thought they could help. As a result, Robert McDonald, a writer and artist who lived nearby, contacted Bill. McDonald told

Bill about a man named Eddie Burks who had had success, and some fame in the national press, for exorcizing a ghost from Coutts & Co, the Queen's bank. McDonald's wife owned an independent television production company, Dove Films, in London, and he wondered if Bill would allow them to film an exorcism at Heol Fanog conducted by Burks. Bill said he was wary of too much publicity and the possibility of it disrupting the children's lives, but he promised to give it some thought. After discussing it with Liz, Bill approached many of the Christians who had helped the family through some of the worst times, and they told him not to allow Burks in the house. Except one, a close friend of the family, who simply said, 'God can work through non-Christians when the time is right.'

By that time, Bill and Liz were getting increasingly desperate as the manifestations around the house multiplied. They called Robert McDonald and said they would be grateful for any help.

*

Bill's testimony: 'It was the same old story after John Aston left. Everything would be fine and we'd be celebrating and then there'd be another problem again and we'd realize it hadn't been sorted out. We were becoming wary again in November 1993 and that's when we got onto our local newspaper and they printed a story about the problems we were having. Robert McDonald read the article and he also read the *Independent on Sunday*, with an article about Eddie Burks and what he had done at Coutts bank. He and his wife wanted to help us out and to make a video about an exorcism that Eddie Burks was involved in. After David Holmwood and John Aston, who were very, very strong Christians, we were wary. Christians have a thing about clairvoyants and spiritualists because of what it says in Deuteronomy in the Bible about people who see the future. Eddie's not a Christian, he's not a medium, he's not a Hindu, he's just… love. A gorgeous man.

'Robert McDonald came down the next day and asked what we were going to do. I said, "We will have to give it a great deal of thought. We don't know who Eddie Burks is. We've had spiritualists here before." Many of those who we knew were

Christians said, "No, no, don't do it – he's not a Christian." One Christian friend, a woman called Brenda, said we should give him a try. By that time we had come to a decision that we had to have someone else. We had to go one step further because we were back in the problems.

'There were so many of these things... things like the woman who walked through the kitchen. Nearly every day there was something, we would see something, out the back, out the front, something up in the studio. It was an everyday occurrence. There'd be a manifestation of some sort or another. But they happened so quickly, and your mind was in such a state at the particular time that you couldn't really tell *exactly* what was there... just that *something* was there.'

*

It took a while to finalize the details with Eddie Burks and the TV company. On 2 January 1994, the Riches' third child Tomas was born, and, in a way, that focus helped them through the hardship, the repeated attacks which left the whole family in tears, the sudden business problems that always returned with the presence.

Finally a date was fixed for Eddie Burks to visit – 13 March. As soon as that happened, the attacks became worse. Before, they had been a constant torment, now they became threatening.

Bill came to terms with that connection on a wet morning in late February. There was no work and the unpaid bills were piling up on the kitchen table. Tomas' crying had prevented him sleeping and the constant pressure of Ben and Rebecca during the day was wearing. At that moment, in the constant gloom of the house, the future looked its bleakest. There was no hope of sorting out the business, of ever having enough money to relax from the constant pressures. He had frittered away all his creativity and he would never complete another painting. And the evil presence would hold sway over their lives for evermore.

He looked up from his brooding and noticed a meat knife lying on the table near his arm. A brief burst of irritation flooded through him. It was razor sharp, and he always insisted it should be kept in a drawer well away from the children. Liz must have forgotten it. With a sigh, he picked it up to put it away, but the moment his fingers closed around its handle he had a sudden thought of how it would feel slicing through the skin on his wrist.

Don't be stupid, he thought. You're not the kind of person to consider suicide.

He shook his head forcefully to remove the thoughts and put the knife in the drawer, slamming it shut with a crash. When he returned to his chair next to the kitchen table, however, he couldn't seem to get the image out of his head. Blood running down his arms. No more problems. Release. He couldn't seem to get rid of the thought of death.

Be positive. Think of Liz and the children. They need you. Focus on the good in your life.

But the terrible thoughts would not go away, until he was swimming in a sea of black despair. Death was all he could consider. And then he sighed wearily and looked down at the table.

And the knife was there once more.

The shock was like a bucket of icy water over his head, yet he felt burning hot inside. He had put the knife away. He remembered the crash of the drawer. He hadn't got it out again. He couldn't have. Surely he would have remembered.

Suddenly terrified, he looked away, but the knife drew his eyes back. The blade, sharp as a razor. It could cut skin easily. It would be over in an instant.

How did it get there?

Suddenly he knew what the house was doing. Gently teasing his thoughts, leading them down a black corridor. It had played its games, its petty torments, but now it was taking it to the next level. It wanted blood. It wanted his life.

'No! You fucking will not do this to me!' Bill roared.

He lashed out with the back of his hand and knocked the knife flying from the table. When Liz came running in to see what was wrong, Bill was leaning forward on his knees with his face buried in his hands.

'Pick it up,' he cried, pointing at the knife. 'For God's sake, pick it up and put it away.'

With trembling fingers, Liz plucked the knife from the floor and shut it in the drawer. When she turned back there were tears in Bill's eyes.

'It wants me to kill myself,' he said. 'We worried about this for so long, Liz, but now I know. It wants our lives. And, God help us, if we don't do something final about this soon, I'm afraid it will get what it wants.'

Chapter 10

Eddie Burks had already received fame and an associated approval of his abilities through several high-profile 'ghost-busting' exercises, as the tabloids called them. A retired scientist, Burks had his roots in the world of rationality, which has consistently dismissed the existence of the paranormal. A childhood psychic experience convinced him there was more to life than what our five senses tell us, yet he managed to put those thoughts to one side throughout his career as a principal scientific officer with the Civil Service. He began taking more notice of them as he approached retirement, and there was one incident in particular that convinced him he had a gift which science could not yet explain.

In 1970, his wife Margaret appeared to him after she'd died of a heart attack, an emotional and intellectual event which had a profound effect. That experience seemed to break the dam, and as he allowed himself to become more attuned to what he was 'feeling' he had more and more psychic flashes, including manifestations of his brother Ernest and son Michael after they had died of illnesses. In 1992 he decided to turn professional, with a brief to take his abilities to a wider audience and explore this fascinating new world he had suddenly discovered.

In December 1993 he embarked on the case that brought him instant widespread recognition. Coutts & Co in the Strand, London, is not renowned for having any truck with anything as insubstantial as the paranormal. It's a place of pinstriped suits, tail-coated doormen, the incomprehensible jargon of the City and the kind of hard-headed approach to affairs which benefits the Queen's banker.

Yet at that time the staff were becomingly increasingly distressed and the management were worried about something that had nothing to do with interest rates, bond issues or the Hang Seng. After decades of mundane calm, the bank's quiet offices had suddenly manifested a ghost. It was headless, like other ghosts of London mythology, and several employees had witnessed it. With it, it seemed to bring a host of tangible disruptions which would be familiar to the Riches. Most notably were power fluctuations that caused lights to flicker on and off, computers to crash and the telephone system to behave wildly. Management had numerous scientific experts trooping through their offices to no avail, and then, with remarkable foresight for such a group of no-nonsense financiers, they considered the possibility of a paranormal explanation; but that's the thing about the business world – where money and the smooth running of the corporation is in danger, anything goes in finding a solution. A few discreet phone calls later, and Eddie Burks was located and invited to the offices.

Burks immediately felt the tinge he associates with the otherworld. He operates by going into a trance, where he allows whatever power is there to speak to him directly, in effect by shutting down his five senses so he can access the other consciousness which so many psychics claim is buried in our minds.

In his vision, the phantom was not headless. Burks 'saw' a tall man with a thin face, dressed in Elizabethan clothes. No witnesses had ever heard the spectre speak, but he spoke to Burks. He was Thomas Howard, 4th Duke of Norfolk, who had been beheaded in 1572 by order of Elizabeth I, and his spirit had become trapped on earth. 'If you can get me from this place, I shall be much obliged,' Eddie reported the spirit saying.

Burks spoke quietly aloud, trying to convince the spirit to move on, and after a while a second spirit appeared, a woman dressed in clothes of the same period. She led the spirit of Thomas Howard into a light that had materialized behind them. Just before he disappeared, Howard turned and thanked Burks for what he had done.

It's a tale filled with all the clichés of ghost stories told before winter fires, almost too fantastic to be true, especially when viewed against Coutts's mundane world of money. Burks is the only witness to what he 'saw', which makes it easy for sceptics to dismiss his claims. Yet there is no discounting the fact that his foray into Coutts worked. All the electrical problems stopped, bizarrely, overnight and the headless phantom was not seen again. Of course, it could be another of the coincidences so beloved of the scientists. Or Eddie Burks could simply be right.

Burks has had many successes since that day, the majority of them unpublicized, many known only to the worried parties who invited him, and the Society for Psychical Research in London. Over time, he has rationalized his gift as best he can and seems to be at peace with his own view. Spirits are often trapped in an 'etheric state', he says. It prevents them realizing the passage of time, and while many spirits move out of this within three days of death, some can stay if strong emotions are suppressed at the time of passing.

Bill Rich was briefed on all of this before Eddie Burks' arrival at Heol Fanog. Nothing seemed incredible to him anymore; he was facing up to the fact that there were no longer any guidelines as to what could or could not be true.

Burks had been carrying out an investigation at Tewksbury in Gloucestershire at the invitation of a friend, Captain John Fergusson-Cuninghame MC, when he heard about Heol Fanog. He returned to his home in Lincoln to meet with Robert and Annie McDonald on 8 March 1994 in order to discuss the possibility of him appearing in their documentary about Heol Fanog. The McDonalds knew of some of the things that had happened to the Riches, but certainly not all. As they chatted, Burks suddenly felt a strange feeling sweep through his body. Then a voice came from nowhere and began to speak to him.

*

Eddie Burks' testimony: 'I was suddenly aware that information was being given to me. This was guidance; it said: "There is much confusion in this situation and it must be approached with caution. Suspend judgement until as much as possible has been expressed in the psychic sense. Some of it is rather dark, but we will help you with this and give you the necessary protection. There are, as suggested, many layers of influence, including the early Celtic, which has some unpleasant overtones. Approach the house circumspectly. Start by appraising the garden. We will lead you, so keep your sensitivity sharp. There will be much of interest in this. That is all."

'Then, after a short interval, I got this: "This is someone in a very agitated state, connected with this matter that we have just been talking about. The new spirit says, 'For God's sake help me, I am in a great tangle, as though I have been wrapped up by a spider. I have managed to break free in order to contact you, but I have a nasty feeling that I am going to be ensnared again.'"

'And then I said, "I think that this the one who was murdered there at the farm." The feeling I got is that he died in the last century. The spirit added: 'You are right. The real story of my death has not been properly told. I came across something that I was not supposed to know. And I was murdered to keep me quiet. I was a fool. I should have kept my mouth shut. But you know what young people are like. If I had been older I would have had more sense. When I passed over, I found myself as though I was in a thicket from which I could not release myself. And every time that I tried to get out, something would happen that contributed to ensnare me again. For God's sake, help me."

'I then interposed: "I can hold him now if I can get him calm. We shall be able to get him away." I think he was fair-haired, and the spirit said, "I was not of this breed, you know," – meaning the local people. I kept seeing him wearing trousers cut off at the knee. Not narrow... they looked like calico. And the shirt was short-sleeved, cut off again around the... well, there again, with brown calico material. He wore an old pair of boots with no socks – bare legs. His personality was rather like someone who rushes in where angels fear to tread. He was killed with a blow to the head. I got an awful pain there at the back of the head. He was hit more than once... an awful pain in my head.

'He emerged to find himself in this thicket. The first blow paralysed his arm. His arms dropped and his knees gave way, but he still showed signs of life so his attacker struck him again. He said there were others involved, but only one man did the deed. He was told to clear off as soon as possible. They did not want to get involved. I got the impression of satanic groups or satanic goings on that he had watched. And he had let it be known – foolish boy.

'I got the feeling of a younger sister he was very fond of, and she of him. I think that she was the one going to come. I said, "He is getting a bit excited himself now – he knows things are moving. He has got to let the pain go at the back of his head. It is part of his memory of the event. I will help him do that. She is calling him. He can hear her voice, but he cannot see her yet. I am a bit puzzled. I am not sure whether the two names are not Annie and Walter. He is standing there and can sense that the light is beginning to grow. And she is standing in the light. She is showing herself as a little girl, as he remembers her. She says, 'Come on, come on.'" He saw her, they went towards each other and embraced. They went forward together into the light.'

*

Following their recent work together, Burks decided to ask Captain Fergusson-Cunumghame to accompany him to Heol Fanog. Burks drove to the Captain's house in Overbury, Gloucestershire, on Saturday evening, 12 March, and he explained to the Captain exactly what had happened during his meeting with Roberts and Annie McDonald. He stressed they had been promised adequate protection during their foray into Heol Fanog, but evil entities would be 'up to all sorts of tricks' against anyone who opposed them. As they drove, Burks told the Captain that a North American Indian guide, with whom he had had previous contact, had materialized in the car – he was there to give them special protection as they were going into a highly dangerous situation.

They drove to Wales on the Sunday morning and Bill met them at the Wellington Hotel in Brecon before guiding them along the obscure route up to Heol Fanog. The house was crowded when they arrived. Gathered in the small kitchen were Liz and the children, Bill and Liz's mothers, Annie and Robert McDonald, and a cameraman who was going to record the event for the planned documentary. They had a cup of tea while Liz ran through the history of everything that had taken place in the house since they had moved in.

After Liz and the grandparents took the children off to Brecon for an hour, Bill led Burks, the Captain and the documentary team around the perimeter fence. They spent most time near the old manor house and buildings, which they all agreed felt particularly evil and threatening.

Halfway around the perimeter, Burks turned to the Captain and whispered that he was acting to a prearranged plan and he was attempting to lay a 'barrier of light' around the place. He then walked around the house, close to the walls, attempting to encircle that in the light too, as he put it.

The documentary team left soon after, and then Bill, the Captain and Burks moved into the kitchen to talk. Bill looked as tense as he felt. Whenever anybody visited to help, it was always emotionally and psychologically draining, but during the days leading up to Burks' arrival, the tension in the house had been almost unbearable.

'Do you want to see around the house now?' Bill asked.

Burks shook his head. 'There is a concentration of energy here, and it is not benign. I don't think that I will have to go any further.' He paused and then added reassuringly, 'This house is being filled with light. I am aware of the figure of Christ…' He closed his eyes and continued, 'I am getting the words: "And there will be nowhere left for them to go. And there will be nowhere left for them to go. So they shall lose fold and fall away. And the light shall prevail. Praise be to God…"'

Then he opened his eyes suddenly and looked at Bill. 'I am aware that close by there is a cross being manifested. First of all it showed itself as dark, and now it is becoming illuminated from within. It is radiating great power and protection. I am told that this cross, which is standing somewhere in front of me, shall be your protection in this house from this point on. The cross is connected to the Christ spirit, which I am sensing is vertically above it.' He closed his eyes again. 'And there is the figure of Christ shedding a light upon this cross, and the words that I am getting are: "And so shall I leave my mark and my protection upon this place. There shall be no more fear and no more darkness and all will be safe within. Praise be to God.'''

When Burks had finished speaking, Bill moistened his lips and said tremulously, 'I think I know what you're talking about. Come with me.'

He took Burks into the living room. On the wall hung the last painting he had completed – *Testimony*, the shining white cross on the turbulent background. The one he had finished in a frenzy without any conscious thought of what he was creating. Burks had never seen it before.

'That's it. That's exactly it,' Burks said quietly. 'It's just what I saw.'

They all stared at it in silence. All Bill could think about were the wild emotions that had raced through him just before he had started work on the picture. At the time he had considered it something negative, a picture borne of anger and frustration. But it hadn't been negative at all. It had come from somewhere deep within him that the darkness had never been able to reach.

*

After they returned to the kitchen and sat down around the table, Burks began to tell Bill what he had done outside the house. 'We put two cordons of light around the house, the effect was to bring in the force that was causing the disturbance. It couldn't escape. It was forced in to within the inner cordon. And then the process continued and the light began to flow as a liquid into Heol Fanog – that is why I felt there was no need to go around the house. There is nowhere left for it to go. It had to let go, and in doing so it fell away into the darkness. The cross was then dedicated as a symbol of your protection from this time on.'

Bill sat back in his chair, almost afraid to believe it was over. 'Does it always work like this?'

Burks shook his head. 'This is the first time that I've worked in this way. It was working on a higher level than the evil entities and I was not meant to make any contact with them. Indeed, it was important that I didn't. I was there to bring the light. I knew when I was coming here – last week when we had the message, I was told that I would be shown what to do. So I didn't plan anything, and it was important that I didn't, because it isn't coming from one's own personality. One should be acting like a servant, really.' He smiled. 'I think that if I were you, I should, as far as possible, try to put the whole thing out of your mind. Try not to dwell on it. Turn your back on everything that has happened and face forward into the light.'

They all sat back in their chairs and rested after the stress of the day. After a while, they realized simultaneously that the mood in the room had changed; it had grown lighter, fresher, as it had done after previous exorcisms. Bill led them from room to room, and they all agreed that the atmosphere of the entire house had changed perceptibly.

Not long after, the rest of the family returned from Brecon. The moment she stepped into the barn, Liz halted suddenly and looked around in wonder. 'What's happened here?' she said. 'It looks so much bigger. There's no feeling of oppression at all. It's gone.'

*

Bill's testimony: 'Eddie had finished his work when he suddenly came into the other room and saw my painting. It was the cross he had seen manifesting itself to deliver the whole situation from evil, in other words from dark to light. And he said, "My God, it looks as if Bill had already thought about it before." That picture itself is so important because it's part of the story… the cross that Eddie Burks saw… and he was the only exorcist who came to the house without any religion. I'm so happy about that because religion's confusing so much. I know we only have to be good and I think God will forgive us for anything. We don't necessarily have to be one thing or another – we only have to be good people. Eddie doesn't regard himself as a spiritualist, or a medium. Obviously he's going around clearing places that are having problems. But he doesn't treat it as a religious experience. So what he did at Heol Fanog was quite remarkable – he finished it, and apparently he was the only person who could.'

*

The day after Burks' visit, the electricity usage in Heol Fanog dipped for the first time. Through all the exorcisms it had remained at the same unfeasibly high level that the Riches had found when they first moved it. Overall, the bill had fallen from around £7 a day to just over £2 – still above average for a house of that size, but as the first substantial reduction, it was a sign that whatever Burks had done had worked.

But not completely. There was still that faint drain, and over the next few days Liz and Bill had several familiar sensations that the darkness which had enshrouded their lives for so long was still there. There was nothing tangible, as there had been before – no apparitions, sounds or smells. It was just a hunch. Bill prayed it was an aberration that would soon reverse itself, but he had been in that position too many times to believe it. Somehow, the thought that it was not all over seemed even worse this time. If Eddie Burks had failed too, with all his previous successes, what hope was there for them? They had tried both religious and secular solutions and nothing had completely cleared the problem. Where did they turn next?

Bill didn't mention his feelings to Liz, but he should have known it was impossible to try to pretend; Liz knew the signs too. Bill walked into the kitchen one day and found her crying gently at the table.

'It's back, isn't it?' she said, through the tears. He nodded, trying to hold back the despair he felt. 'But it's different too,' Liz added curiously. 'I can feel the evil thing in the background… that black cloud, God help us… but there's something else too. Outside…a feeling… God, I can't put it into words!'

She looked at Bill for support, but all he could do was shake his head and shrug. 'I don't know, Liz. We've always felt it in different ways. I think I'm going to call Eddie.'

Burks was surprised his exorcism had not been a complete success, but he suggested Bill and Liz wait a while before deciding that things had returned to their previous terrible state; sites were often in upheaval for a while after an exorcism, he said, like the aftershocks that followed a major earthquake. However, he did warn them that the spiritual purity of the house since it had been cleansed could attract other lost souls from around the area.

'If you see anything, don't be afraid,' he explained. 'They're simply trying to find their way to where they have to go. Heol Fanog will be like a beacon to an earthbound spirit. They will be drawn to a place in your garden where they will be able to pass over.'

As they spoke Burks suddenly realized that it wasn't completely over. Something had remained after the exorcism – he could feel it, in the kitchen, just a few paces from Bill.

*

Bill's testimony: 'The electricity dropped significantly after Eddie's visit and that had never, ever happened before when any of the other people had come to do similar things. Eddie had certainly come across this problem before. He explained that it was the spiritual atmosphere that was taking the electricity and taking energy from us.

'I phoned Eddie up to explain my doubts and he said, "What can you see, then?" And I said, "It's not what I can see, it's what I think." He went into this type of spirit or trance and suddenly he saw something. He said to me, "I can see a young man wandering around the kitchen wringing his hands. This is the man who did the murder." Eddie didn't know anything about how the murder had happened – that the victim had been hit in the back of the head with an axe – I hadn't mentioned a word of it to him. But Eddie felt a tremendous pain in the back of his head. And the spirit was saying, "You're not listening to me." Meaning me – Bill. Eddie said he felt the man had been told that if he carried out the murder he would be quickly taken away and he wouldn't have to worry about anything else. And in fact the murderer was arrested and brought to Brecon jail where he was hung. And this was the soul appealing for release.

'Eddie kept on saying that the poor spirit was so tormented because he had been made an assurance by the people who had asked him to do the murder. Bearing in mind that the victim of the murder was a man who had seen too much, about black magic. And this poor spirit who was in torment kept thinking, I'm going to be alright. Everything's going to be alright. They *told* me everything's going to be alright. The spirit was going to the gallows and Eddie was reliving the poor young man's last emotions, his last thoughts, and it was being repeated to me on the telephone. Eddie woke the moment when the noose went round his neck and he explained it to me then. He said the young man knew at the moment of his death that they were going to let him die and he'd never said a word in his trial about this. Eddie did his thing to free the spirit and eventually he said it was gone – the house was clear.'

*

As the weeks passed, they began to feel Eddie Burks was right; the sense of being watched and the oppressive malignancy which had filled every corner of Heol Fanog never reached its previous intensity, although it was always there, stalking in the background, refusing to let them forget it. It may simply have been that their minds were focused on new horrors.

*

Liz's cry brought Bill sprinting down from his studio, taking the stairs two at a time. The children were all having a noon rest and she had been alone in the kitchen, reading. Bill found her standing in the middle of the room, shaking, her face drained of blood, her arms clutched tightly around her.

'Lord, what is it?' Bill put his own arms around her. 'Calm down,' he whispered. 'Tell me what happened.'

'I saw…' The words choked in her throat. 'I saw a man, but –'

'A spirit?'

She nodded. 'God it was horrible. It looked like he'd been in a car crash. Half his face was missing. There was blood all over him, and wounds. He looked dazed, like he didn't know where he was or where he was going.' She swallowed noisily. 'He passed through here and went out there.'

Bill followed her pointing finger out through the window into the back garden, which was wet and leaf-strewn with the onset of autumn. There was nothing there, although he didn't expect to see anything. In his mind he tried to picture the kind of horrific apparition that could have disturbed Liz so much after all she had experienced in Heol Fanog.

'And it went into the garden,' he murmured. 'Just like Eddie said.'

'He was right – it wasn't threatening. It wasn't even concerned that I was there. But it was bloody frightening.'

'The way Eddie described it, we should see it as something good,' Bill continued. 'Lost souls finally making their way home.'

'Why here?' Liz said, suddenly bursting into tears. 'Haven't we been through enough? I can't take it anymore, Bill.'

He hugged her tighter, but he couldn't find any words to say. He felt on the verge of physical and mental exhaustion too. It had been going on so long, and he didn't want to be part of that world any longer. On their meandering route away from the mundane world, they had stepped off the path and now it seemed like they would never find their way back again.

*

Over the months through winter and into the beginning of spring, Bill and Liz were haunted as they had never been before. It was just as Eddie Burks had described; the apparitions seemed to be passing through and they never saw any of them more than once. There was an old lady and an old man, a child and several middle-aged men and women, all of them bewildered, all of them seemingly making their way into the garden. Their dog Beau used to love rooting in the garden, but he became more and more reluctant as the phenomena increased, until eventually he wouldn't go out the back at all. Bill would put him out, but he would simply howl and dash around the side of the house to the front.

The Riches didn't find the experience terrifying; there was no sense of evil in the apparitions at all, just an uncomfortable mixture of sadness and incomprehension. After their great fear at the presence that used to be in Heol Fanog, Bill and Liz could cope with the ghosts – they were just a glimpse or a shimmer across the room – but the regularity of the sightings was disturbing, and it prevented them reclaiming any hope of a normal life.

The one bright spot was that Laurence started to visit regularly. He was nothing like the child that had left Heol Fanog so many months ago; he was calm, lively, reassured, and he would take Beau for long walks and play with his brothers and sister. Bill remarked to Liz, 'He's a wonderful son. I'm so proud of him. Seeing him like that gives me some hope that we can be alright as a family again.'

But when he went away, they were left with the gloom and the ghosts, and at one point they almost broke. There was an afternoon when they simply sat hugging each other, fighting back the tears. 'I don't want to see these things anymore,' Bill said, expressing Liz's exact thoughts. 'I want to go back to a normal life and paint and do normal things. I don't want to have weird people trooping through the house talking about spirits and ley lines and curses. *I just want a normal life!*'

Soon after, the electricity drain began to creep up slowly, Bill's business took its mysterious but familiar turn for the worse, and the mood of the house altered perceptibly, like thunder was approaching. They reacted quickly. Bill phoned Eddie Burks and said, 'It's starting to get bad again. We can't face it getting back to how it was. Come now, please, and end it once and for all.'

*

Burks arrived on 8 June 1995 with Ralph Noyes, Maurice Grosse and Montague Keen, three members of the Society for Psychical Research, an esteemed London-based organization with a long history of careful investigation into the paranormal. As usual, Liz took the children away so the exorcism wouldn't frighten them. When Bill greeted the visitors, a part of him was sure it was their last chance. He didn't dare consider what would happen if they failed.

The tension in the house was tremendous. Montague Keen clicked on the tape recorder as everyone held their breath and watched Eddie Burks. Slowly, he walked around the room with his eyes closed, breathing deeply, trying to feel the vibrations that emanated from the stones of Heol Fanog. For what seemed an interminable period, nothing happened, and then Bill noticed a slight but perceptible change sweep over his face like a dark cloud. He reached behind him to touch his back curiously. 'This contact in the small of my back… I suppose this would be the solar plexus chakra… it usually indicates to me that it's a low-level entity.'

Burks sat down, bolt upright, rocked slightly, then rose sharply and walked around the room before returning to the chair. His breath was laboured. Bill shivered, trying to *feel* the atmosphere himself. Was it the demonic presence that had terrified them for so long?

'I'm not picking up any personality at the moment.' A long pause. 'I'll have to get up and walk around again.'

Bill shifted anxiously. Burks returned to the chair, his breathing even heavier.

'At the moment I'm tending to confirm Liz's impression that this is something shadowy. There is no impression of personality at all so far. Normally at this stage I would be aware of personality. It's not that it's just elusive – it's that there is nothing to be elusive. I have got to somehow identify this… to get to grips with it.'

Silence descended once more. Through the open window they could hear the sound of the trees swaying in the breeze and smell the heated air carrying the perfume of the fruit trees and herbs in the garden.

'I think a sense of urgency arises from a prompting, perhaps at another level, that something has to be done about this thing,' Burks began slowly. 'I think this thing… this creature, elemental or whatever – I shall get a clearer idea later – it's got to be rendered inoperative. Dissolved. Dispersed. And that is probably the right term. So I'm going to ask for help in this procedure. It's probably angelic… it may be human-spiritual, the nature of the help, but whatever responds, I'll do my best to follow it through.'

Through his anxiety, Bill tried to follow what was happening. Burks seemed to be reaching out for something with every fibre of his being; his body trembled, his entire attention focused inward. As Bill watched, Burks' face grew darker, more troubled. The atmosphere slowly took on a syrupy quality until Bill found it difficult to breathe. In that instant, he knew. The thing that had haunted them for so long was there.

'I'm getting some sense now about what we're dealing with,' Burks continued in a low, steady voice. 'It's very ancient. It preceded events about which we know. It even preceded the black magic rituals which took place prior to the murder in the middle of the last century. There's a quality here which is very primitive… sacrificial… It's been aroused or resuscitated by events. It needs to be resuscitated because it needs to be dispersed. It's been lying dormant for several thousand years. I suspect, but I don't know for sure, that it's Celtic, ritualistic, sacrificial…'

His voice trailed off. He was panting like he was undergoing some terrible exertion and his hands gripped each other until his long, thin fingers grew white.

'It may be necessary to get a clearer idea of its origin. I think we have to know what it is we are dealing with a little more closely.'

Bill felt this body fill with tension. The choking atmosphere was electric and chill, despite the hot wind blowing through the window. Nervously, he glanced around the room. *Where is it? Jesus, protect us.*

'Oh, this is interesting,' Burks exclaimed with a sudden release of the tension in his body. 'It has some quality of something I've not met in this form before – a quality of what I would call naturist, related to the misuse of natural forces. It arose originally through Celtic nature worship of a corrupt sort and was invoked, I think, by a Celtic priesthood in a bad phase. Yes, it is… It has got an animalistic aspect to it. I want to get close enough to it to identify it without getting so close that I become identified with it, and I don't particularly want to do that.'

The brief crackle of stress in his voice frightened Bill. He had a sudden vertiginous sense of the power of the thing, and he knew why Burks did not want to associate with it too closely.

'I think it was originally invoked to create mischief against those who were proscribed in some way.' His voice had grown calm again. Bill was amazed at how composed he remained. 'Maybe other tribes, maybe other persons. And it would have struck terror into them. The power of striking terror is now considerably reduced because this is a different culture and won't respond. It is in a sense programmed, but it has enough of its original purpose left to cause trouble, but mercifully not as bad as it would have done had we been in sympathy with the culture of the day.'

He paused. Bill waited anxiously.

'So it is pre-Christian. It does not respond to Christian methods, but I think it must be dealt with by the exercise of a particular aspect of love and light that is synonymous with it.'

Burks seemed to draw something up from within himself; he closed his eyes and put his head back.

'I am being guided to take my mind back – the power of imagination back – to the time of its generation and to invoke the beast that was in the Celtic priestly tradition at the time, because this will be recognized by this creature. I don't know how this is going to work, but I shall do what I'm prompted to do. It has to be disarmed and dispersed back into the natural kingdom, removing from it the Celtic human element which was the evil aspect of it. In other words, this is a reversal process, but it must be done gently, not with spite or malice.'

Bill couldn't see anything, but he could feel it; in the tingle of his fingers, the tightness of his chest, the pressure at the base of his skull. He muttered a prayer to Jesus. Perhaps it was just Eddie Burks' words creating an image of tremendous struggle between the light and the dark, but he felt that at any moment something would break through.

'I think the love that is being brought to play will neutralize the evil, and also will break the bondage, and what is left has to be dissolved into the Kingdom of Nature,' Burks continued in his soothing voice. 'We can now bring ourselves forward in time to the Christian era and invoke the love of Christ and the power of angelic Kingdom to eradicate all traces –'

There was a crackle of power which blasted through the tape recorder. Bill looked at it anxiously. The noise had sounded like a gunshot in the still of the room; and it hadn't been natural. It was like a lightning bolt had surged into it, and then out in the blink of an eye.

Burks was still talking quietly, ignoring the interruption. 'The Christ that was invoked on an earlier occasion last year, as well as here on an earlier occasion, is still here and is responding to a request for help in the cleansing of this area, and the Christ presence is making itself felt.'

The room grew noticeably brighter as if another light source had been illuminated. Bill's rational mind searched for answers; just the sun breaking through the branches of the trees? The tension seemed to shift too. As his muscles unknotted, Bill became aware of the ache in his shoulders as if he had been carrying a sack of coal. There *was* something happening.

'There is a peace coming into this room and into this house, a relaxation of tension,' Burks said, as if he had read Bill's thoughts. 'I am going to go out of this now. I think I have done the work that's needed.' He breathed deeply and then spoke to the room at large. 'There are one or two points I would like to make. I think that the entity – for want of a better word – that was here has been dormant for a very long time. It was pre-Christian as we have already seen, and as such did not recognize the power of what was done here originally. One important lesson in dealing with something of this sort is to identify its origins, and any remedial action has to pay respect to those origins. The Christian aspect can be brought into play.' He gave another deep breath and added softly, 'I think I will let the thing rest now.'

*

Afterwards, they discussed what Burks claimed to have found. His description of some powerful evil force conjured by Celtic tribes before the birth of Christ gelled with what others had said about a pagan origin to the numerous terrors that had assailed Heol Fanog. Bill knew that many who heard about Burks' explanation for the long, arduous nightmare would dismiss it as unbelievable, but to him it was no more incredible than disembodied footsteps, figures appearing from nowhere, electricity disappearing into the ether. It was just a matter of perspective.

The proof, he knew, would be in the effectiveness of Burks' exorcism. Was it finally over?

*

As of March 1996 there has been no resurgence of any strange phenomena. From the morning after Eddie Burks' departure, Heol Fanog's bill was less than the average for a house that size and after six years of disappearing power it seemed too much of a coincidence to attribute it to anything else. Bill's work picked up instantly; orders suddenly started to creep in, an agent called with an offer to take him on, without any action on Bill's part. The children became better behaved, the house lighter. Laurence continued to visit with increasing regularity. He got on with Bill as well as he ever had done and developed a strong, almost sibling, relationship with Liz. His games with Ben, Rebecca and Tomas lasted for hours. No one mentioned how he had been after the footsteps were first heard. Laurence's own feelings on whether he was possessed, as Bill averred, were a secret; he wouldn't even discuss them with his father. He simply saw it as the most troubled time in his life, but now it was behind him, he didn't want to consider the causes.

It seemed like old times.

*

Autumn comes quickly to that part of Wales, sweeping the brilliant yellows and greens from the canvas, spreading around muddy browns, murky purples and greys, with the occasional smattering of gold and red. The garden had been unbearably hot all summer, but right then it was cool and pleasant. Liz stood with Tomas in her arms and Bill at her side as they watched Ben and Rebecca play with an old car near the barn.

'What do you think?' she whispered after they had watched in silence for several minutes.

'I don't know.' Bill thought for a long time before continuing. 'I'm almost afraid to say it.' Then: 'This time I think it's gone. You can feel it. The house has never felt this good since that day we moved in.'

'Even so,' Liz added quickly. 'I don't want to stay here.'

'No. I think that's a good idea. The work is picking up, your mother has offered to help out with a loan… we should be able to find somewhere new pretty soon.'

'What was it, Bill?' Liz was almost afraid to discuss it in case it brought it all back. 'What have we suffered with for the past six years? Some Celtic spirit, like Eddie says? The devil? What?'

'It was evil. Does it need another name? But we've beaten it now, thank the Lord, and what we've been through has given us a different view of the world – not a very nice one, and certainly a frightening one – but I think we've had our eyes opened, and I think we'll come out of this the better for it. Eventually.'

'I can't think that at the moment, Bill. It's still too close.'

'Soon,' he said, slipping an arm around her waist. 'Soon.'

*

Bill's final testimony: 'I don't want people to think of us as in any way eccentric. Naturally, you are in your life what you do. If you are a painter, you don't look like a clerk, you don't look like a businessman. What we have tried to do is be as clear as we could, bearing in mind that something really has happened. People have heard of hauntings and things, but this was not just a haunting. To understand this, you've got to be us, you've got to live us, you've got to get into that. Something inexplicable and evil happened in this house, but it didn't start when we moved in. It was there before. But the evil we came across made us, with help, know Jesus, and for that, I have to say, it was worth it.'

Liz's final testimony: 'There have been so many bad times in Heol Fanog, but relatively recently it's been so hard to hold it all together. Because it's very wearing being an actress twenty-four hours a day, because throughout all this there's never been a moment of allowing emotions to come through, because of the children. I once broke down in tears when I had to go to my mother's because it was so bad in the house, and I'd never seen their little faces as frightened as then, and I swore I'd never do it again. Recently there's been the worry of money. The worry of, is the house OK? Might it come back? For so long, we couldn't move… It's so hard to hold on now. I'm finding it very, very hard. It's taken a toll, this actress trick, and maybe that's what people will say when they read this book: "God, I couldn't have gone through something like that. I'd have had a breakdown." Some people do and some people don't, and I didn't.

'I refused to admit the things I saw or felt or experienced. They can't be true. How can they be true? Even though I know they are – you can pretend. I think it's called a state of denial. Now though – relatively soon – I think there's going to be a way out. Away. This is the end, this book, of the experience. Our faith in Jesus grows day by day and I feel he will rebuild our lives. Once we've given our testimonies to what happened, I hope we can put it all behind us. For good. For ever.'

Endwords

You have just visited a place where none of the rules of your life hold sway. It would be easy to dismiss it because it is *so* detached from the mundane reality most of us move around in during our day-to-day lives. I think that would be a mistake. Wrapped up in whatever happened in Heol Fanog is a fundamental question that we should all ask ourselves. It runs through science, philosophy and religion. It concerns the way in which we live our lives. It is, simply: Is this all there is?

Here is a glimpse into the lives of a couple who believe they have experienced something remarkable and which has changed them in many ways. I have spoken to almost everyone connected with the case in an attempt to provide a wide perspective on what happened. Now it is up to the reader to decide how far they want to progress into the mysteries of that lonely Welsh house: a simple step into the almost-accepted world of hauntings, or a full-scale plunge into the realm of demonic beings. All the evidence has been presented for your perusal. There is no proof that would convince a scientist, no tricks that can be duplicated in a laboratory, no reams of equations or banks of data. But there is the kind of evidence that would be presented in a court of law - the evidence of human beings witnessing and then reporting. They have been interrogated and their testimonies placed before the jury. If this was a court of law, the judge would sum up everything the jury has heard from the prosecution and defence, so I will attempt to provide an overview without letting my opinions cloud the issue.

The first thing you have to consider is the credibility of the central witnesses – Bill and Liz Rich. Their lifestyle and their beliefs may not be yours, but if you were on a jury that would be irrelevant. Are they honest, upstanding people? Yes, certainly. It is here that you will have to take on board my testimony. I have spent time with them at their home and I have spoken to them for hours on the telephone. I have interviewed neighbours, friends, acquaintances, doctors, lawyers and school teachers, all who have had some connection with the Riches and all of whom will attest they are ‘good people’. They have a lot of love, not only for each other and their children, but also for anyone else they can help out. They are hard-working, their house is scrupulously clean and their children are well-cared for and polite. Since the events in Heol Fanog they have become ardent Christians, although they held many of the tenets of the religion long before they attached themselves to a church. Their reasons for doing this book were not financial; I approached them and had to persuade them to help me. They simply wanted to unburden themselves and to show the world that ‘these things happen’.

The Riches were certainly vulnerable during their time in Heol Fanog. The collapse of Bill’s marriage, his attempt to introduce his beloved son Laurence into a new relationship, Liz’s twelve-year-long battle with anorexia, all served to place them under intense psychological stress, whether they acknowledged that fact or not. Raising your children is very stressful when it’s taking place in a peaceful, stable atmosphere, never mind when you’re suffering dire financial problems.

While in this vulnerable state, Bill and Liz repeatedly had their equilibrium shaken by attacks, which were not all from the supernatural realm. The moment they opened themselves up to help, they were besieged by people with a spiritual axe to grind. Lost in a world they didn’t understand, they were thrown this way and that by those who claimed to be able to read the signposts. It resulted in the very foundation of their life being kicked away. At the time, the Riches certainly took comfort from all help given, but whether it was effective, or even advantageous in the long term, is debatable. I would never suggest that any of these visitors were anything but wholly innocent in their motives – I am sure they believed completely in what they did. Nevertheless, and with understatement, there are some occasions where I feel their help may have been misguided.

But to suggest that any of this warped the Riches’ minds enough to make them fantasize all the things they saw, heard, smelled and felt in Heol Fanog is too simplistic. They may have made connections between incidents of bad luck that weren’t there – and they did have a phenomenal amount of bad luck in Heol Fanog – but the sheer weight of the phenomena they experienced seems to defy any criticism that it was 'all in the mind'.

There were so many paranormal events in Heol Fanog during the time the Riches were there that I have not been able to detail them all. In the early days there were minor things...books and other small objects turning up in different parts of the house to where they had been left: once, a life-size cardboard figure moved across Bill's studio overnight. Towards the end, the manifestations were appearing on an almost daily basis. Bill and Liz have kept a detailed record of everything that happened in the form of notes and recordings, which shows them moving from curiosity through bewilderment to outright terror.

Then we have the other witnesses to the phenomena who have put their testimonies on record – a previous resident, the dog warden, all the spiritual leaders. Were they all lying, misguided, or the victims of some strange brain defect?

To say this was all some delusion is actually *more* unbelievable than to accept that something terrible and beyond the bounds of reason happened in Heol Fanog between May 1989 and June 1995, and, indeed, before that time.

If we can believe that strange things did take place in that house, the next step would be to decide exactly what did happen and how far one should extend the boundaries of the phenomena. The various physical manifestations are easy to categorize, but the situation becomes more hazy when one considers less tangible things, like the staggering bad luck the Riches suffered; business collapse, dying or blighted pets, repeatedly failing cars, illnesses. The Riches believe the house and what it contained jinxed them in a very direct, malignant way. Living in that atmosphere, day in, day out, they were convinced they were under attack on a whole range of levels. A business collapse in isolation is simply that. Yet if it is only part of a catalogue of misfortune, when does it stop beyond mere coincidence?

Sometimes when you're researching a book or an article there is a pile-up of synchronicity as information comes out of the blue which adds to or enlightens the work in progress. The poet Robert Graves experienced it many times while working on his book *The White Goddess*, and in the end there were so many coincidences he felt he was being pushed in a particular direction by an unseen hand.

He is quoted in Colin Wilson's boundary-breaking book *The Occult:* '"Chains of more than coincidence happen so often in my life that if I am forbidden to call them supernatural hauntings, I must call them a habit."'

My own impression of Heol Fanog is that it is certainly a peculiar place, with an atmosphere quite unlike anywhere else I have visited. I arrived on a bright sunlit day, after the final exorcism. Bill and Liz claimed it was a different place to the house they had suffered for so long – brighter, friendlier. If that was the case, it must have been a particularly terrible residence before, for I found the atmosphere quite oppressive. There is a sense of claustrophobia in the expansive garden. The ruins of the old manor house have an uncomfortable air about them. One still has a prickly feeling in the house itself. I would not live there.

The breadth of weird phenomena in the house was almost too wide to pinpoint the cause. It wasn't simply a haunting, or a case of demonic possession: according to those who visited the place, it was both, and more. Yet there are several areas that the mixed bag of investigators agree on independently. Dowsers, spiritualists and Christians were all convinced the toilet-hallway area was the focal point of the malign atmosphere. The spiritualists and the Christians identified three haunting spirits – an old woman and two young men. They also agreed on a fourth, some satanic angel and which Eddie Burks, who finally cleared the house, felt was some Celtic-era evil force. Many people can accept the existence of ghosts, but they understandably find it hard to step into the seemingly fantastic realm of demonic beings. It's a little too Hammer Horror for many. Bill and Liz are both adamant there was an evil intelligence at work in the house; they (along with the minister David Holmwood) witnessed the inhuman form. Unusually tall, black, with a hook-nose or beak – three people, the same description.

I was particularly interested in two areas during my investigation. Firstly, the Egyptian connection. Both Bill and Liz mentioned their experience in the Pyramid of Cheops as a defining moment when they first felt there was 'something else'. Whatever they sensed in the dark tunnel, it terrified them and forced them to flee into the light. Left at that, it could be dismissed as a singular case of the goosebumps. However, the Egyptian influences continued throughout their stay at Heol Fanog. Dr John Aston's advisor described seeing an Egyptian design, the swathing of a mummy, before even knowing about Bill and Liz's story. There was the Egyptian-style amulet discovered in Cowbridge, which gave Bill an electric shock when he picked it up. And then there was that beaked figure which Bill described as being like the Egyptian Falcon-god Horus. As a codicil, it should be noted that Bill's great grandmother was a committed Egyptologist and able to read hieroglyphs. More coincidence? Or did something make contact with them in the Pyramid of Cheops… something which followed them back home?

Then there is the matter of the ley lines. Scientists will tell you they don't exist, but when three independent dowsers can go to a property and pinpoint the same line, something is happening. What they are is a different matter. The interesting thing is that the dowsers claimed Heol Fanog was the worst example they had ever discovered of 'negative geomantic forces', and at the same time the house contained some of the worst and most concentrated examples of supernatural phenomena. Many dowsers believe haunted houses lie on 'black streams' or negative leys, but beyond this the cause and effect becomes muddied. Are the hauntings a physical by-product of these mysterious energies – sensory hallucinations of some kind caused by…magnetic anomalies, or some other physical phenomenon? Or are there such things as spirits that are attracted to these spots because of those energies?

The evidence of the upstanding members of the clergy and the lay people is adamant that there was a supernatural presence in Heol Fanog. Why, then, were the Riches susceptible to such sustained horrors when the previous tenant had only mild experience? The answer here, you could suggest, is a simple fact of life: the strong pick on the weak. As we have established, Bill and Liz were at low points in their lives and hoping to make a fresh start. Their defences were down, their hearts and minds laid bare: easy prey.

I would contend that the location of the house was also an issue. In its isolation, every problem was focused within and then magnified, weakening the inhabitants' psychological defences further. If Bill and Liz had friendly, helpful neighbours packed closely on all sides, with whom they interacted regularly, would they have suffered so much?

And then there was that seething creative energy which must have filled the house: Bill's intense drive to paint, unable to gain vent as he was consistently rebuffed by circumstance, financial problems, children. How much negativity did that generate?

In the end, it's not as important to understand exactly what happened in Heol Fanog as it is to simply accept that something did happen.

In the testimonies of all those immediately involved with the house, there was direct contact with the supernatural. And it wasn't just a quick glimpse through the doorway, it was a long, lingering look that terrified all those who were forced to see. The level of emotion evoked in those who passed through Heol Fanog should give you some pause for thought. These weren't hysterical people. Imagine what it would take to cause such charged passion and fear.

Put yourself in their place. Then say nothing happened, it was all in the mind…

At a lecture in Birmingham, while I was preparing this book, a member of the audience wryly queried me about Bill and Liz's case before stating firmly that he was an 'unbeliever'. Afterwards, his partner quietly admitted several of the Rich family's experiences had happened to her in a house in the Black Country. The man was brought to an immediate halt because he couldn't say his partner was stupid, crazy, misguided or irrational; he knew her. In fact, he thought she was as rational as he was.

At the same lecture, a member of the audience had to leave the room in a state of distress. The moment I started to talk about Heol Fanog, he saw the dark figure of a man in ancient costume appear behind me. It unnerved me, certainly, but then strange things are occurring every day, in every town, in every street…

And unlike what the moralistic ghost stories tell us, the events at Heol Fanog aren't some kind of punishment from the unknown for bad people. If you decide to believe the testimonies in this book, consider: they could happen to anyone, at any time, in moments of weakness. You. Me. For no other reason than that our defences are down. And as reasoning beings it is that lack of reason which is terrifying. Random terrors that can destroy our lives without cause – it's just not fair. Bill and Liz were victims. If their case is true, we could all be victims.

The author's notes follow this message.

If you enjoyed this book, if it inspired you, enthralled you or in any slight way enriched your life, please, please tell everyone you know…family and friends, share your enthusiasm on Facebook and Twitter, write a review on Amazon or Goodreads, stop a stranger in the street and tell them. The rules of publishing have changed and in this brave new world, no author can survive without the support of vocal readers who can spread the word. Help the writers you enjoy keep working on the words you love. They need you!

And if you want to build your relationship with the author of this book, there are plenty of places you can go.

You can find out more about Mark, and read his blog, at: www.markchadbourn.co.uk

You can follow his news at www.facebook.com/ageofmisrule or communicate with him directly on Twitter: @Chadbourn

Find Mark easily on Goodreads and see what he's reading, or check out his photography on Instagram where he goes under the name Chadbourn.

On Tumblr, where he generally blogs about screenwriting, you can find him at Chadbourn.tumblr.com while on Google+ you can find him at plus.google.com/+MarkchadbournCoUk/about

New Mark Chadbourn ebooks coming shortly from Emerald Eye:

THE ETERNAL

A shocking supernatural thriller. Annie Bolton's future was bright - until she met the Eternal, an immortal cursed to wander the Earth bringing death and destruction. Only Annie and a mysterious drifter - a human who has pursued the Eternal across continents - hold the key to stopping the triumph of evil.

SCISSORMAN

The Age of Misrule begins here! When burned out moneyman Jon Summers moves into his sprawling childhood home, Arcadia, he makes a shocking discovery – a doorway, perhaps, to another world, the source of all fairytales, all myths, all legends. It seems magical…until something terrifying comes through that door into modern-day London. Part supernatural thriller, part fantasy, part dark fairytale, this book was shortlisted for the British Fantasy Best Novel Award.

LORD OF SILENCE

In the magical city of Idriss, a mysterious place isolated at the heart of a forest which seems to go on forever, Vidar is a man tormented - by a lost memory and a vampiric jewel that demands the life energy of others. Now, with a killer loose within his home city, Vidar must solve a three thousand year old religious mystery to unlock the terrifying secrets of his own past. A dazzling fantasy. A murder mystery. A puzzle for the reader to solve. Lord of Silence is all of these things.

THE FAIRY FELLER'S MASTER STROKE

The British Fantasy Award-winning story finally available in ebook! A strange and disturbing painting hangs in a London art gallery. Its secrets may unlock the mysteries surrounding the life of a troubled young man, if only he can decipher them. But when he embarks on a quest to uncover the obsessions that gripped the painting's insane creator, Richard Dadd, he finds himself in a terrifying world. In his introduction to the original story, acclaimed fantasy author Neil Gaiman said: "Mark Chadbourn gives us a novella, in which the painting is a clue (perhaps), a murder-weapon (possibly), and above all, and unquestionably, a key: a key to a life, to a family, to mysteries, to solutions, to madness and to, above all, reality. It's a story of a life wasted, of love and of pain, and of a place in which Dadd's painting and Dadd's life become both a template and an excuse: a reason for living, and a reason for dying, and it is not until the very end that we understand what we have read."

SUNSHINE AND SHADOWS

AUTHOR'S NOTES

As I write this, the year is winding down. The sun never climbs high above the horizon. Chill breezes blow, leaves fly. I live in the middle of a forest, in an old house with a lot of history. It's not a place for people who are easily spooked. When the trees are bare as they are now, and the wind is lashing through the high branches while night comes down hard, there's a very old part of our brain that stirs. It doesn't matter how rational we are, or how rooted in our age of technology, we still hear voices in the whine of the gale in the eaves, or see faces hovering in the interplay of moonlight and shadow away in the woods.

It seems an age since I first visited Heol Fanog. It was a hot summer's day and the old house was flooded with sunlight. But that ancient part of my brain still kicked into life. When I walked up the path with Bill Rich, watching him get assailed by several wasps that came nowhere near me, I couldn't help but think of all the old, familiar stories of the supernatural, where 'cursed' people are caught up in something they can't explain or control. That's the thing about superstition – we're predisposed to allow it entry to our lives, and once it's there it's like a cut that we keep worrying at until it throbs and takes over our thoughts.

Or, to take a different approach, when you engage with superstition, you take a walk into the deep woods and leave civilization far behind. You go to a world where the trees and the woodland creatures speak. It's a place where you learn more about yourself and the deep currents that move you, move all of us, the world inside rather than the world out there.

I'm sure there are a lot of people who would like to think this entire story is a work of fiction, the kind of yarn I spin in my novels. It's not. I was a journalist before I became a novelist, and I have digital recordings and contemporaneous shorthand notes for every single interview included in this book, and plenty more that I didn't include. There's also a short report of the strange events at Heol Fanog in a BBC Wales news programme, and the original report in The Independent newspaper that sparked my initial interest, if anyone would like to search them out. There is no doubt that the 'account' has a foothold in reality.

Plenty more people will no doubt believe that Bill and Liz Rich made everything up. I'm not here to convince anyone. I called the book *Testimony* for a reason – it's a disparate group of people talking about their subjective experiences. But I will say this: I found Bill and Liz decent-hearted people who clearly did not get into this for their own financial gain. Most of the time they seemed bewildered by what was going on around them. They just wanted their lives back. They also signed a statement – a photograph of which was included in the original book publication of Testimony – swearing to the veracity of their account. During our many chats, I didn't personally think they were a couple of liars, and in my time as a journalist I have interviewed a lot of politicians.

Also consider that this story isn't just about the Richs. That was the great attraction for me as a writer. Many people had experiences in Heol Fanog that they couldn't explain (including a few that I didn't include in the book, for space or to avoid repetition). I've heard some pretty unpleasant responses to this. Everyone is a liar. Everyone is crazy or stupid. If you have a particular worldview, one that refuses to be shaken, it's understandable to look for other explanations. But to attack those who tell their stories – who didn't have to tell them, and often didn't want to speak out – just seems so mean-spirited. And let's be level-headed here: *everyone* is lying? *Everyone* is crazy?

All the men and women I interviewed certainly believe something odd was going on at Heol Fanog – it may well not be what they *thought* was happening, but we'll never find out what truly did unnerve them if we don't begin to accept them as honest if baffled people. But if you do take these disparate stories at face value, the question of what was wrong with that isolated house becomes truly unnerving. The sheer weight of all the accounts coming from different mouths, different lives, can't be easily swept away. Something happened there. But what? We all have to make up our own minds by weighing those testimonies.

Yesterday I set out on a walk through the forest, along an abandoned train track, past an old canal and ruined Victorian buildings. I usually take a few photos on my phone. The changeable weather presents something new every day, transforming places I've stumbled across a thousand times. There's a lot of magic round here, however you want to interpret that word. I encountered a couple of people on my trek, a regular occurrence. Sometimes it's familiar faces. This day it was strangers exploring the wild locale. We got talking, and once they found out I was a writer, they opened up about their own stories, as people always do. One told me of hearing the growls of a dog in their house late at night, and smelling its musk in regular 'hot-spots' every now and then – they'd never owned a pet. The other discussed receiving a phone call from a relative who, they later discovered, had died earlier that day – a strange, garbled call, of repeating, baffled questions. "Where am I? Where am I?'

Everyone has an interesting life, once you drill below the surface. Both of them had had strange, inexplicable experiences that they wanted to discuss, because they wanted to make sense of it themselves. They weren't unusual. Nearly everyone I meet on these regular walks has something lurking in their past – a ghost, a light in the sky, a cursed object. Try it yourself. Ask random people to open up. You'll soon discover that many, many of them have a story to tell. They've often kept it to themselves, or pushed it aside because it *couldn't possibly have happened.* You start to realize that this world is stranger than we ever think – all these people nursing secret, weird stories that never break the surface of the usual scrutiny of society. In every country, in every town, perhaps in every street.

I had my own experience a couple of years before I met Bill and Liz Rich. Late one night I was in the bathroom of another house, a 250-year-old cottage that used to belong to the village blacksmith. Suddenly I was jolted by the thunder of heavy feet running along the landing. I dashed out to find no one there – the house was empty. A year later my sister revealed that she'd had the same experience when she was visiting and in the house alone. And a year later, when I sold the old place, I was told by a neighbour that everyone in the village *knew the house was haunted.* Nobody ever mentioned a word while I was there. Silence. Secrecy. These stories simmer behind closed doors.

In this time of technological marvels, a part of us needs the numinous and mysterious more and more. It's a refuge from the desperate, grinding reality of everyday life, a place where we can dig deep into our unconscious and reflect on who we are and our place in the world.

I haven't spoken to Bill and Liz in a long time, but I know they're still living in the Brecon area. Heol Fanog is still there too. It's hard to locate. There are no sign-posts, the roads are narrow and it's so isolated you won't come across anyone to give you directions. But if you're determined to find it, you'll get there. Just make sure it doesn't find you too.

ABOUT THE AUTHOR

Mark Chadbourn is an award-winning author, a screenwriter for BBC TV Drama and a former newspaper and magazine journalist reporting from across the world. Raised in the UK East Midlands, he studied Economic History at the University of Leeds before beginning his journalistic career. His writing has appeared in almost all UK national newspapers, including The Guardian and The Times, as well as several magazines. His novels have been published in the US, Japan, France, Germany, Norway, the Czech Republic, Poland and across the Commonwealth. He is a two-time winner of the prestigious British Fantasy Award, for his novella The Fairy Feller's Master Stroke based on the painting by Richard Dadd, and for his short story, Whisper Lane. The Dadd novella resulted in an invitation to lecture at Tate Britain.

Made in United States
Troutdale, OR
05/25/2024